Confronting Life's Challenges
Sermons on the Struggles We Face

W. Douglas Hood, Jr.
Greg Rapier
John C. Randolph

Foreword by Thomas K. Tewell

Parson's Porch Books

Confronting Life's Challenges: Sermons on the Struggles We Face
ISBN: Softcover 978-1-951472-69-6
Copyright © 2020 by W. Douglas Hood, Jr., Greg Rapier, and John C. Randolph

www.parsonsporch.com

Confronting Life's Challenges

Table of Contents

Sermons by John C. Randolph

Foreword

When St. Augustine was asked the purpose of a sermon, he thought back to what Cicero, the Roman statesman, said about oratory. The purpose of a sermon, St. Augustine said, is to teach, to delight and to persuade. The book of sermons you hold in your hand accomplishes all three. I should know. I read every word of these sermons. As I did so, I learned invaluable spiritual principles about the ways of God; I delighted in the anecdotes, stories and metaphors, and most importantly, I was persuaded to walk closer to Jesus Christ. It is not hyperbole to say that these sermons by Doug Hood, Greg Rapier and John "Skip" Randolph, represent some of the finest weekly preaching in the United States today. A big statement, But it is true! St. Augustine is smiling in the Kingdom of Heaven.

Ask members of First Presbyterian Church of Delray Beach Florida what they like about their church and you will receive a myriad of answers. Some will comment on the sublime music or the outstanding Christian Education programs for children, youth, and adults. Others will describe the caring fellowship in the newly remodeled facility, while others will affirm the outreach to the local community. But, everyone mentions the preaching! The sermons at First Presbyterian Church of Delray Beach make the Bible come to life! Hundreds and hundreds of people come to each worship service anticipating that they will hear a "Word from the Lord" in these tumultuous times. This is not only the opinion of those who live in South Florida, but also those who worship on the internet from literally all over the world!

I must tell you that it is quite unusual for three preachers of the quality of Doug, Greg, and Skip to preach regularly from the same pulpit. The fact that they are all associated with First Presbyterian of Delray Beach, Florida, is a testament to the strong leadership of the Senior Pastor, Doug Hood. Doug has purposefully surrounded himself with gifted preachers who bring out the best in him, even as he brings out the best in Greg and Skip. As a result of this excellence in preaching, First Presbyterian of Delray Beach is an enigma among mainline Protestant congregations in America: it is growing. It is growing in every measurable way: in worship attendance, on- line presence, membership, financial giving and volunteer time, but most importantly, in discipleship. People all over America, and the world, are experiencing the life changing presence of the Lord Jesus Christ in the worship services and sermons! Is it any wonder that so many people want to be a part of this special church family in Delray Beach, even from around the world?

In these challenging days when we are living through a pandemic that has gripped our world, as well as racial tensions and protests in a divided nation, this is a book whose time is now. Aptly titled, *Confronting Life's Challenges: Sermons on the Struggles We Face*, these sermons are practical to the core. They do not shy away from the tough questions and perplexing issues which confront us each day. Instead, they urge us to focus on God as we face real-life issues of anxiety and anger, guilt and grief, doubt and despair. Our preachers instruct us to open our eyes, by faith, and see the presence of God in our midst!

Some years ago, First Presbyterian Church of Delray Beach established a Distinguished Preacher Series that brought such well-known preachers as Tom Long and Barbara Brown Taylor to South Florida. It is a great honor for me to have preached in this series myself. Before my sermon, I told the Delray Beach congregation, to sustained applause, that they do not need a Distinguished Preacher Series because they already have a Distinguished Preacher in Doug Hood. After the applause subsided, I told Doug, in front of the congregation, that he must pay me more for these compliments!

After reading this book and getting better acquainted with the sermons of my new friend, Greg Rapier and, my long-time friend, Skip Randolph, I realize that the Delray Beach congregation has been blessed with not one, or two, but three distinguished preachers.

But, the one you will meet in these sermons is not any of these preachers, as outstanding as they are. The one you will meet is none other than the Savior himself! Although the style of each preacher is distinctly his own, the one quality that characterizes each of these preachers is that they continually point to Jesus!

Welcome to an Adventure in Discipleship as you discover the one who can help us meet, and overcome, the challenges of life and the struggles we face!

With anticipation for what God has in store for us as we read these sermons again and again,

Tom Tewell
Claremont, California
August 2020

Preface

"Preach the word. Be ready to do it whether it is convenient or inconvenient."
2 Timothy 4:2

Harry Emerson Fosdick and Johnston Ross, colleagues at Union Theological Seminary in New York City, were once having a friendly debate over the most effective place to begin a sermon. Ross argued for the Bible, making a careful exposition of a particular passage and moving toward application for present living. Fosdick argued for the opposite direction, beginning with the conscious need of his audience and moving toward a final solution that is found in the pages of Scripture. It is a little like a conversation I recently had with my travel agent when booking a Viking River Cruise: I wanted to begin in Paris and conclude in Zurich. The agent persuaded me that beginning in Zurich and concluding in Paris would be more enjoyable.

My own preaching takes its direction from Harry Emerson Fosdick. Actually, that is not completely accurate. Though I tend to move in the same direction that Fosdick advocates, my approach to preaching was deeply influenced by the friendship and mentoring of Bryant M. Kirkland, formerly pastor of The Fifth Avenue Presbyterian Church, New York City. Kirkland shared with me that effective preaching demands careful listening: listening to the conversations of ordinary people in the community where the pastor takes up the vocation of weekly preaching. Such conversations reveal the problems and concerns that are uppermost in the minds of the people. Begin there, said Dr. Kirkland. Begin where the people are located as they sit down on Sunday morning. Begin with their struggles.

With force and clarity, the Apostle Paul writes, "Preach the word. Be ready to do it whether it is convenient or inconvenient." It seems that from generation to generation one voice, one summons, is heard again and again. It is that the single greatest and most pressing need is for the people to be equipped for interpreting the nature and purposes of God to our troubling time. The great Scottish preacher and teacher, Peter Taylor Forsyth (1848-1921) once made that very argument in his lectures before Yale Divinity School. Persuasively,

Forsyth argued that the first business of the preacher is to equip the Church to preach Christ to the world. "The Church is the great preacher", says Forsyth. The person who stands in the pulpit week after week has the duty to give the Church the words for their preaching.

Presently I serve the pulpit of the First Presbyterian Church of Delray Beach with one of the finest preachers I have known, Greg Rapier. As I write these words, Greg has just completed two years of ordained ministry. Yet, his excellence in the pulpit is that of a more seasoned preacher. Additionally, eight years ago it was my good fortune to welcome as guests to worship at First, Delray Beach, Mr. and Mrs. John and Leslie Randolph. "Skip" as his friends know him, is recognized as one of the finest attorneys in South Florida. He is also a man of deep faith who has studied preaching at my alma mater, Columbia Theological Seminary, Decatur, Georgia. Skip's deep faith, humility, and warmth sparkles when he stands before a congregation in the pulpit. Appreciated widely by the congregation, Skip is a frequent guest preacher of First, Delray Beach. This small volume of sermons includes not only my sermons preached from the pulpit of First, Delray Beach, but also sermons from Greg Rapier and Skip Randolph.

It takes time to be a Christian. Consciously spending time with God through daily reading of the Bible and prayer is a non-negotiable. "Train yourself for the holy life," says the Apostle Paul. As you do this day upon day an uncommon power from without will shape and form you. It is the work of the Holy Spirit. Deeply formed into the image of Christ you will feel a compulsion to share with others what is happening to you, share how you are being transformed from the inside out. That is the preaching of which Forsyth spoke. The desire, which lay behind my vocation as a Christian minister, is to equip ordinary people for extraordinary preaching of the Gospel of Jesus Christ. For this hope, I present this small collection of sermons from the pulpit of First Presbyterian Church of Delray Beach.

W. Douglas Hood, Jr.

A Special Word

Fred Craddock, identified as one of the finest preachers in the world by a study of Baylor University, once remarked that creativity does not take place in a vacuum. The application of that comment to preachers is that great preachers read the work of great preachers. Great preachers look over the shoulders of great preachers to observe their approach to responsible engagement of the Bible's truths to the present day, to observe the helpful construction of a message that communicates well, and to capture images and illustrations that may continue to illumine God's word today. Each of the authors of this small volume read deeply the work of other preachers. Naturally, where we make a direct observation to another's work, that is noted in the sermon or in the endnotes. Nevertheless, to Craddock's point, such exposure to the work of others shapes our own thoughts and means of expression. It should be no surprise that one Christmas Eve, after I had completed my message, a visitor to the church that evening approached me and asked, "Have you heard of Tom Tewell? You sounded just like him this evening."

W. Douglas Hood, Jr.

Acknowledgments

After Robert J. McCracken, a preacher of another generation, passed his seventeenth birthday, he went to his father and told him that he would like to become a minister. There was a long pause after which the father made two remarks. One I mention here, "If you get into a pulpit be sure to select a great text." Arguably, that is sound counsel. I would offer a second, "Identify a great preacher, not to imitate, but one who will challenge you to great heights in the craft of preaching as you identify your own unique voice in the pulpit." For two of the contributors of this small collection of sermons, John Randolph and me, one of those great preachers is Thomas K. Tewell. He stands in the small company of two other preachers, Barbara Brown Taylor and Thomas G. Long, who continue to inspire and instruct us in the craft of preaching. All three have stood in the pulpit of the First Presbyterian Church of Delray Beach as a guest of our Distinguished Preacher Series. Mr. Randolph, Rev. Rapier, and I are honored that Tom Tewell has provided the Foreword to this volume of sermons.

The membership of the First Presbyterian Church of Delray Beach, Delray Beach, Florida has welcomed our preaching, encouraged us through emails, written notes, and telephone calls. Sharing God's word from the pulpit of that great community of faith has been a wondrous journey. Wondrous because of the holy privilege and sacred responsibility of communicating the Gospel to such an intelligent people who challenge our own thinking, stretch our own imaginations, and demand from us our best preparation as we seek to demonstrate the claim of an ancient text, the Bible, as the living voice of God today.

Furthermore, these sermons could not have been published without the dedication, support, and administrative care of Nancy Fine, Business Administrator of First Presbyterian Church of Delray Beach. She has typed, proof read, and made multiple suggestions that have improved this work. Unquestionably, this volume is stronger for Nancy for which the authors are in her debt. More, Nancy remains a trusted and appreciated colleague in my ministry.

Most importantly, each author is deeply grateful to our spouses, Grace Hood, Lissette Rapier, and Leslie Randolph, each who offer unfailing support and encouragement to our shared ministry. The Lord's truths, wisdom, and immeasurable love always come through each of you. It's easy to preach when the Gospel is richly experienced in the homes each of you make for us.

W. Douglas Hood, Jr.

Sermons by
W. Douglas Hood, Jr.

W. Douglas Hood, Jr. has been the Senior Pastor of the First Presbyterian Church of Delray Beach, Florida since 2012. He holds a Master of Divinity from Columbia Theological Seminary and a Doctor of Ministry from Fuller Theological Seminary. Doug was the 2015 Moderator of the Presbytery of Tropical Florida and was a commissioner to his denomination's General Assembly in 2014 and 2016. He is the author of *Nurture Faith: Five Minute Meditations to Strengthen Your Walk with Christ*. Doug is married to Grace, has two children, Nathanael and Rachael, and resides in Boynton Beach, Florida.

Are You Anxious?
Matthew 6:25-34

Listen for God's Word

"Therefore, stop worrying about tomorrow, because tomorrow will worry about itself. Each day has enough trouble of its own."
Matthew 6:34

As I sat down this week to prepare the message that is before you I remembered a story shared with me as a child. Perhaps you heard the same story. The story of a clock that decided to stop ticking. It seems that one day this clock began to think about how many times it would have to tick that year. It added up to over thirty-one million times. The clock became anxious and overwhelmed. Thirty-one million times was a lot, more than the clock could emotionally manage. The clock gave up. It decided to quit, abandoning the profession of being a clock. One day someone reminded the clock that it did not have to tick all thirty-one million times at once. All that was required and expected was that the clock would just tick one tick at a time. That would be enough. Calm restored, the clock reengaged and began once again to keep time.

How many of us are overwhelmed like that clock? We think about the number of friends and family members that are close to us and they each have problems. Their difficulties add up to thirty-one million. We are overwhelmed caring for them. Then there are our own needs. We are overwhelmed. We grow anxious. Just like the clock, we just want to quit. The story of the clock teaches us that we do not have to tackle all thirty-one million problems at once. Only one difficulty at a time. This morning's message is about anxiety. It is a struggle common to all of us. This week, I looked deeply into this text, reading the reflections from liberal scholars and conservative scholars. Additionally, I listened to over thirty-two years of ministry, of people coming into my office and sharing with me how they faced anxiety positively. I have gathered three things that I want to share with you: three observations that may help you with the challenges of anxiety. Not one of these may be new to you. The three things that I offer may be tools you have already found.

That great Christian thinker, C.S. Lewis once said that there are times when the people of God simply need to be reminded rather than instructed, times when we simply need to be reminded of what we already know rather than to be instructed on something new.

The first thing that I want to share with those wrestling with anxiety is that you need to travel lightly. I learned this when I went to serve a congregation in Texas in 1994. Shortly after my arrival at a congregation in Irving, Texas, a member that congregation took me aside and shared with me that he had three daughters. He would introduce me to two of his daughters but he could not introduce me to his third daughter. That is because she had died at a young age. He shared that this daughter was so alive, so loving, and so caring. She embraced everyone that she met warmly. Then she became very ill. Doctors could do little and in a short time, she was gone.

He shared with me that prior to his daughter's illness, he was anxious about many things. The company he had worked with for over twenty years was now in the midst of a major restructuring. He was against every one of the changes. He went to management and he let management know that he was against all the restructuring. They listened but demonstrated that they were not interested in his ideas. The restructuring proceeded as planned. His residential community was under the authority of a Homeowner's Association. Major changes were placed before the homeowners for consideration. He found himself in the minority opposing the changes. His neighbor, only two homes from his own, began making some landscaping decisions that he disagreed with. He shared his concerns with his neighbor, that he felt the changes in landscaping did not fit the community. The neighbor listened respectfully. Finally, the neighbor ignored the helpful suggestions and proceeded as planned. The anxiety only increased. The church also contributed to his anxiety. It is 1990 and the Presbyterian Church has published a new Hymnal. The red hymnbook that had been in service to the church for decades was replaced. This man simply did not like the new hymnbook. You may remember that *Readers Digest* even commented on the new hymnal with a very unhelpful article. The article stirred resistance to the hymnal by pointing out that it no longer had the hymn, Onward Christian Soldiers. Naturally, he voiced his concern to the governing board of the church, but to no avail. The blue hymnal was now in the church.

Anxiety over his work place, his residential community, his neighbors' landscaping decisions, and the new church hymnal consumed him. Then, his daughter became ill. Suddenly, that was all that mattered. He poured all of his energy into helping her overcome her illness only to see her die.

Remarkably, over time, he began to appreciate the landscaping changes his neighbor made and begin to borrow some of his ideas. He also decided to trust the leadership board of the church and the decision to replace the church hymnal. In fact, he simply decided to stop fighting every change in his life and to travel the road of life lightly. His concerns were now limited to loving his daughters and his wife. He stopped carrying a suitcase of concerns and reduced his baggage to a carryon.

The second thing that I share with you is to listen deeply to the words of Christ here in Matthew. Christ teaches us to worry about today only and let tomorrow take care of itself. That is Christ teaching us to balance our mental budget. Many of us are going into mental and emotional overdraft. That is because we are gathering all the problems of tomorrow, and next week, and next month, and next year, and we are placing them before us today. That is precisely what the clock did, counted all the times it would tick in one year and worried about all of them at once. None of us has sufficient funds to cover it all. We go into overdraft when we pay attention to today's problems and tomorrow's. Matthew tells us to let tomorrows' problems take care of themselves tomorrow. I have a pastor friend who has two adult sons, both married. Both have children. One son is an alcoholic. When he realized that his drinking problem threatened to cost him his marriage and his relationship with his children, he sought help. As is common with people in Alcoholics Anonymous, some experience multiple failures before a sustained period of sobriety. They fall down and get back up. Finally, the day came when he took his last drink. On the second anniversary of sobriety, he received a call from his father. His father congratulated the son for beating alcoholism. If you have struggled with alcoholism or you have a family member or friend who struggles with alcoholism, you can imagine the son's response.

"Thank you, dad, for your love and support. Moreover, thank you for remembering that this is the second anniversary of my sobriety. However, I do not know if I have beat this disease and neither do you. What I ask for, dad, is that you pray with me right now, over the phone, that I will go to bed tonight and fall asleep without taking a drink. My only concern is for today. Tomorrow I will fight tomorrow." We must balance our mental budget and fight today what is before us today. Let tomorrow fight tomorrows' difficulties.

The third thing that I would share with you from the reading of Scripture and listening to congregations for thirty-two years is that we need to learn to rest our souls in God: to take those things that trouble our minds and make us anxious and to bring them to God and rest in the power of God.

I heard a wonderful story some years ago of a mother that trusted her little daughter to walk to grocery store for a loaf of bread. The store was close to home and a short walk. The mother gave her daughter some money and reminded her that they had walked there together many times. "Would you walk to the store and purchase a loaf of bread before dinner?" The daughter was so pleased her mother trusted her to go to the store by herself. With money in hand, the little girl left the house for the store. The mother knew how long a walk to the store should be. When the little girl did not return in a reasonable period, the mother grew anxious. After looking out the window multiple times, the mother was just about to call the police when her daughter appeared at the door. The mother asked her daughter what took so long. She simply answered, "I was helping my friend, Debbie, from down the street". Seems that Debbie had accidently broken her doll. "She loved that doll so much. So I helped her." "You helped her? What could you have possibly done to help Debbie with her broken doll?" asked the mother. "I helped her cry". Do not ever minimize the power of simply sitting with someone who is broken, crying with them. This is what Scriptures calls us to do: to take our brokenness and place it in the care of Almighty God who cries with us and embraces us with God's love.

After my friend in Texas lost his daughter, he began to travel lightly. He had difficulty understanding why a God of love would allow his little girl to die. We all share this difficulty. However, he did not stop his wife and his two daughters from going to church. Moreover, they did so every week. However, he was unable to go. After his wife and his two daughters dressed and went to church, he would work around the house. This continued for almost a year when one day, on a Friday, the mother dressed the two daughters for church. As they were heading out the door and he said, "Sweetheart this is Friday. Where you going?" His wife answered, "This is Good Friday. We are going to the Good Friday services". After his family walked out the door, he began to remember the significance of Good Friday. It is the day when God watched a world inflict unimaginable cruelty upon his boy. It is a day when God watched this world nail his boy to a cross and simply left him there to die. "It was then I realized, for the first time, that though I don't understand the cross, and I certainly don't understand at all how God could let my little girl die, at least God knows the pain to lose a child. I also realized that the best way to honor the legacy of my little girl was to love deeply as she did. I started going back to church. I still did not understand why God allowed my little girl to die. Yet, I now understand that God had suffered as I did. God also had a child taken from him. More, three days later God raised that boy back up to life once again. It is then I realized that God is not yet done here on earth. Therefore, I have returned to church and returned to being useful to God. I do not understand much about God and my faith. I have many questions. Perhaps, just perhaps, somewhere along the journey of life, the answers will come to me."

As we were sitting together talking, I noticed on his coffee table the blue Presbyterian Hymnal, the new hymnal that was causing him so much anxiety. I did not say anything but he clearly knew what was on my mind. My curiosity was unmistakable. "I'm still angry they took out <u>Onward Christian Soldiers</u>," he told me. "However, there are some new hymns in that hymnbook that I really like. I found some new favorite ones. I purchased a copy so that my two girls and my wife and I can sing one of the new hymns together at night before we go to bed. I guess it was not such a bad decision after all, the publishing of a new hymnbook. Moreover, I now trust God more, particularly in those times I simply do not understand". May it be so for you and for me. Amen.

Are You Overwhelmed?
Acts 12:24

Listen for God's Word

"God's word continued to grow and increase."
Acts 12:24

The late Pittsburgh astronomer, John Brashear, wrote his own epitaph: "I have loved the stars too fondly to ever be fearful of the night." What a beautiful and encouraging thought! As I have pondered those words over the years since I heard them, it seems to me Peter, one of Jesus' disciples, could have written them. As Jesus' disciple, Peter did not always live in the sunlight. Peter's ministry was not always filled with the brightness of success and victory. Peter knew days of darkness and despair. He knew times of trouble and tragedy. Here, in the twelfth chapter of Acts, we learn that King Herod has begun to make life difficult for the Christian Church. James, John's brother, is killed with a sword. Then Herod has Peter arrested and placed in prison. What is remarkable is that Herod then places sixteen guards on duty simply to watch Peter! Then notice what happens next. The Church begins to pray for Peter. In the midst of trouble and difficulty, the Church does what it does best; the Church clings to hope.

I wish we had access to Peter's thoughts while he was chained in prison. Did Peter ever doubt the ministry that he has now given his life to? Did Peter ever question the existence of God when things became really difficult for the Church and for him? The Church of Jesus Christ is now under a most severe persecution and its continued existence seems doubtful. King Herod is on a rampage to stamp-out the Church by destroying its leaders. Disciples are either being killed or placed in prison and the Church is under constant attack and is being scattered everywhere. The night is very dark and it seems that Peter must be feeling overwhelmed.

The day that is described in this chapter of Acts is not unlike today. On our streets, in our neighborhoods, and our places of work, the prevailing mood of the day is, overwhelmed. The world today seems to be more complex, more massive, and more unmanageable than our individual and corporate memory can recall. The magnitude of the problems we face as a nation, particularly the gun violence we have seen in the past two years, leave us exhausted and frightened. It seems that we are up against a new level of massiveness and everything now appears to be beyond the power of ordinary people and governments to solve or control. Confronted with the overwhelming complexities of life today, the question presses against our hearts and spirits, is there hope?

What is disappointing to me is that we have no record in Scripture of Peter asking these questions or doubting his call from God. If Peter ever felt overwhelmed by the circumstances of his day, as we feel overwhelmed by the circumstances of our day, there is simply no record of it. What the Bible does tell us is that after Peter was chained and placed in prison, with sixteen guards watching him, Peter simply went to sleep. And, the Church held onto hope. The Church prayed.

When we are in a dark place on our journey, hurt because we are frightened by the senseless evil we see in our own communities, disappointed by people who don't share our political or religious convictions, or angry at people who don't seem to do what we believe is the right thing, we face a great choice that will determine the rest of our journey. If you choose to remain frightened and angry, you are essentially choosing to always be overwhelmed and to be a victim. It does not matter where else you go, or how the news may change from day to day, or what people may do or fail to do. You will continue to position yourself to always be overwhelmed: to always be powerless and helpless. But, look at the Church here in Acts. The Church refuses to give-in, to become powerless, to be a victim, and to abandon hope!

In his autobiography, *The Long Walk to Freedom*, Nelson Mandela said that in his twenty-seven long years in a South African prison, the singing of the prisoners was essential to his ability to survive. That is because as they sang, the prisoners protested that their souls were still free. A prison cell and chains cannot imprison the human spirit. That can only be done when we abandon hope.

When we gather in this beautiful Sanctuary week after week, coming in from an uncertain and dangerous world, and open our hymnbooks and sing, <u>To God Be the Glory</u>, as we did this morning, we are not pretending that everything "out there" is okay. We are making a holy protest against the evil "out there." We are announcing that there is still God and that God is present and active in ways we may not always be able to see. And, when we close our worship with the hymn, <u>Called as Partners in Christ's Service</u>, we are stepping forward and announcing that we intend to be used by God in a mighty way to change what is now unacceptable in the world.

Peter is in chains, guarded by sixteen soldiers and the Church prays. The Church refuses to give-in, to give-up and to be powerless. In his book, *Facing Death*, Billy Graham shares a story about Donald Grey Barnhouse, one of America's leading Bible teachers in the first half of the 20th century. Cancer took Barnhouse's first wife, leaving him with three children, all under twelve. The day of the funeral, Barnhouse and his children were driving to the service when a large truck passed them, casting a noticeable shadow across their car. Turning to his oldest daughter, who was staring sadly out the window, Barnhouse asked, "Tell me sweetheart, would you rather be run over by that truck or its shadow?" Looking curiously at her father, she replied, "By the shadow, I guess. It can't hurt you." Speaking to all his children, Barnhouse said, "Your mother has not been overridden by death, but by the shadow of death, that is nothing to fear."

As a Church, as members of the body of Christ, we have a moral and faithful obligation to reevaluate our mood. Since the world tends to magnify the negative, a Christian mood of hope is vital. When someone asks, "What is this world coming to?" the Church must answer, "Christ has come into the world." It is that response that changes the prevailing mood. It may not be within our power to control the news or the conditions of life, but we do have a choice for our attitude toward them. The world is hungry today for the witness of the Church in a time like ours. The church's high calling is to strengthen people by our unwavering confidence that, in the midst of unsettling news, God is not absent. Amen.

Are You Caught in Despair?
John 10:7-17

Listen for God's Word

"I am the good shepherd. I know my own sheep and they know me, just as the Father knows me and I know the Father. I give up my life for the sheep."
John 10:14, 15

There are people who cling very tightly to the past. They are unable to let go. They hold on beyond anything that is reasonable. Consequently, they are unable to live fully in the present. The result is despair: despair for what is lost.

Then there are others who teach us another path. An old man is lying in his bed. He is surrounded by his wife, daughter, and four grandchildren. His breath comes slowly now. When silence stretched to an unbearable length, the youngest granddaughter throws herself on the bed and cries, "Oh, grandpa, grandpa, don't leave us." The man slowly moves his hand to take hers and says lovingly, "Let me go. It's peaceful there."

A great tragedy of life is that there are some who never hear the great message of the Old and New Testament, the news that we have a God who is a shepherd who covers us with grace and gently leads us into God's future for us. That is the message the Church has for a frightened world: a world that clings too tightly to the past. God extends the shepherd's hand to lead us into a future that is bright with God's promises. What is required is that we learn to recognize the hand of the shepherd and to trust it. God is a shepherd who, in the person of Jesus Christ, has walked before us, knows the future and will accompany us on the journey. More, Jesus is the great shepherd who has personally experienced loss, and brokenness, and fear, and yet, found his way forward.

This is the message the Church has to share with the world: a message of hope. It is not a message of optimism. It is not a message that life will be free of disappointments, failures, and brokenness. It is a message of hope.

27

What is the difference? Look at our Bible lesson carefully. Jesus self-identifies as a shepherd. When sheep become lost or injured, a shepherd cares for them and shows them the way forward. Despair is the inability to move forward. The shepherd moves us forward. We don't have to stay stuck; we don't have to be a prisoner of the past.

Winston Churchill said that if the present quarrels with the past there can be no future. That is to say that we cannot move forward until we let go of the past. Some churches have difficulty understanding this. Just this week, I spoke with a national church consultant who said he was working with a church in a large city. The church has a rich and proud past but is seeking help with moving forward. As he began work with them as a consultant, he tasked them with developing a campaign slogan. What they came back with was, "Preserving Our Past." The consultant predicts that they have less than five years of ministry remaining. Yet, this consultant is also working with another congregation that has an equally rich past and tradition. They too were tasked with thinking deeply about a campaign slogan for their long-range strategic initiative. They came back to the consultant with one word, "NEXT." That is a church that has every promise of a vital, dynamic ministry for years to come. Winston Churchill is correct. If the present quarrels with the past, there can be no future.

Perhaps you are familiar with the Roman god, Janus, from which the month of January is named. Janus has two faces; one face looks back to the year that has passed with despair and sorrow. The second face looks forward into the new year with hope and anticipation. The shepherd, Jesus Christ changes our face from despair to hope and anticipation. Despair is refusing to let go of the past: past hopes, past dreams, and past relationships. The dying grandfather understood that peace was in moving forward.

In my second year of theological studies, I was given a most remarkable opportunity though I did not immediately understand it as such. I was asked by the Dean of Students to move out of my dorm room and into the home of a retired professor who had never married. Dr. Ludwig Dewitz had been professor of Old Testament and Hebrew Language for many years at Columbia Theological

Seminary in Decatur, Georgia. He was a man deeply admired by the faculty and administration of the seminary. Yet his reputation among students was somewhat different. Legendary were stories of Dr. Dewitz becoming exasperated at unprepared students and throwing a piece of chalk at them. His aim was remarkably accurate. There seemed to be an unusual calm that came over the campus at his retirement.

Dr. Dewitz had now suffered a stroke and lost the use of his right hand and arm. Doctors advised the seminary administration, the only family Dr. Dewitz had, that someone would be required to move in with him for the first four months of his rehabilitative care. The faculty nominated me. Knowing only the legend of the man, I declined. I am ashamed to say that my "no" became a "yes" when I was further told that I would receive a stipend of $100 per week and the removal of all room and board charges from my graduate bill. The relationship I developed with Dr. Dewitz became one of the most meaningful of my life.

He introduced me to the opera and Masterpiece Theater; concerned that I was not sufficiently appreciative of the arts. He cultivated a deep love for the Old Testament that I did not previously have. More, he showed me what it meant to trust the hand of the shepherd, Jesus Christ.

Early after I had moved in, I asked Dr. Dewitz, "What's it like? What's it like to lose the use of a hand and arm?" His answer taught me much, "You speak as if I am stuck. I am not stuck. I simply have a difficulty to overcome." He proceeded to tell me that his car was now in the garage being specially equipped for one-hand drivers. He pointed to the piano bench where he had just received in the mail music for one-hand piano. Dr. Dewitz had no time to lament what is now lost; what he once had but was now in the past. Dr. Dewitz was not stuck. With the help of his shepherd, Jesus Christ, he was moving forward. Despair believes that you are stuck. The good shepherd comes to move us forward.

Some years ago, the wonderful preacher John Claypool shared with me this story. One clear day an Italian peasant met a Roman Catholic monk who had come down a mountain; down from a monastery atop the mountain. The peasant asked the monk what the men of God who lived in the monastery did day after day. "What do us men of God do up there on the mountain top day after day? I'll tell you what we do. We fall down, skin our knees and then we get back up. We fall down, skin our knees and then we get back up. We fall down, skin our knees and then we get back up. We all belong to the Society of Skinned Knees. But, we know that when we fall, the hand of the shepherd is there to grasp us and place us back on our feet and move us forward. You must learn to recognize the hand of the shepherd. Then, you must trust it. It is the hand that leads from despair to God's future for each of us." Amen.

Are You Disappointed?
Deuteronomy 34:4

Listen for God's Word

> *"'I have shown it to you with your own eyes; however,*
> *you will not cross over into it.'"*
> Deuteronomy 34:4c

This is a remarkable picture of Moses! He is at the point of death, on a mountaintop, gazing out over the Promised Land, a land for which he led God's people to possess, pondering God's word to him that he himself will never enter the land. A universal truth of life is captured in this tragic moment, a truth that neither the great or small among us escapes; life brings equal capacity to experience joy as well as disappointment. This singular moment of Moses' life lays hold of our imagination as no other moment in his life does. Life sometimes falls short of what is desired and for which we intended our labors to provide.

That moment is on the horizon for every one of us: that moment when we realize that our grandest dreams and the greatest desires of our heart may not be realized. Moses wanted to cross over into God's Promised Land and the Apostle Paul urgently wanted to take the Gospel to Bithynia. Both were denied. Both their circumstances and own earnest efforts gave Moses and Paul every reason to believe their central purpose and passion in life would be achieved. But, what would lie beyond their vision was the disheartening experience of watching their dreams tumble to the ground, "I have shown it to you with your own eyes; however, you will not cross over into it."

Phillips Brooks, a preacher of another generation, has established himself as one of the great Christian preachers of any generation. There is a life-size, bronze sculpture of Brooks in Boston where he completed his ministry. Brooks is the author of that great Christmas hymn, O Little Town of Bethlehem. Nevertheless, Phillips Brooks did not plan to be a preacher. That was his second choice. He planned to be a teacher. That was his great aspiration in life. Graduating from college, he plunged into his chosen profession of

31

teaching and he failed. He failed completely. After Brooks was dismissed from his teaching position, Brooks wrote in a letter, "I don't know what will become of me and I don't care much." Brooks was struggling under the weight of a devastating disappointment!

In a sense, Brooks never recovered from the disappointment. Let me explain. Once he picked himself up from the disappointment of failure, Brooks entered seminary to prepare for the ministry. Once ordained, his ministry flourished! During his ministry in Boston, Brooks received a letter from a small tailor shop near his church. It read, "Dear Dr. Brooks, I am a tailor in a little shop near your church. Whenever I have the opportunity I always go to hear you preach. Each time I hear you preach I seem to forget all about you, for you make me think of God." It is said that of all the letters Brooks received during his ministry that was the one he cherished the most.

But, listen to this. Brooks became known as such an effective communicator he was invited to a meeting with the President of Harvard University. According to witnesses, Brooks left that meeting trembling and white as a sheet. He had just declined an invitation to teach at Harvard University! He declined because of that letter from a tailor and so many like it. Brooks now knew that God intended him for the pulpit.

Barbara Brown Taylor is a preacher of considerable distinction of the present generation. Many of you heard her when she was a guest in our Distinguished Preacher Series a number of years ago. What you may not know is that she did not intend to be a preacher. That was her second choice. Barbara Brown Taylor's heart desire was to be a novelist. She completed two novels, searched and searched for a publisher and was repeatedly turned away. Like Phillips Brooks, Taylor entered seminary to prepare for the ministry. Years later, she would be distinguished by *Newsweek Magazine* as one of the twelve most effective preachers in the world, *Time Magazine* identified Barbara Brown Taylor as one of the one hundred most influential people of the world and her books on Christian faith consistently sit on the New York Times' Best Seller List.

What are we to make of these stories? They demonstrate what many of us have already experienced in our personal lives; that few people have a chance to live their lives on the basis of their first choice. We don't have access to Moses' inner thoughts as he sat upon that mountain, looking out over the Promised Land. Paul speaks little of his failed ambition to preach in Bithynia. What we do know is that both Moses and Paul had a choice to make, the same choice that confronted Phillips Brooks and Barbara Brown Taylor. They could look back bitterly, questioning where it all went wrong, angrily regretting that they ever had dreams at all, and this decision producing tears of disappointment. Or, they could hold their heads up in their disappointment and acknowledge that God has blessed their labor, that in their struggle, God's purposes were advanced and that by God's power, they did step closer to eternal things.

Viktor Frankl, who survived the Nazi concentration camps, wrote, *Man's Search For Meaning.* In this book, Frankl claims that in the camps he learned the last of all human freedoms that can never be taken away is to choose your response to anything. So, no matter how small the ration of bread was that he received, Frankl always chose to give some of it away to another starving prisoner. In doing that, Frankl chose to remain a human being, and he chose not to be a victim.

Moses was not a victim. He is honored to this day as one of the great leaders of Israel. Paul was not a victim. Because he kept his mind alert to God's work, even in the midst of his disappointment of not entering Bithynia, he heard God's call to Macedonia. Biblical scholars assert that had Paul not gone to Macedonia, we would never have heard of Paul today. The chain of events that began to fall into place for Paul as a result of traveling to Macedonia, rather than Bithynia, resulted in nearly two-thirds of the New Testament being written.

Moses, and Paul, and Phillips Brooks, and Barbara Brown Taylor are "nevertheless" people. They did not receive their first choice. "Nevertheless" they kept their eye on God. When you say, "nevertheless" after disappointment, you are placing yourself in the hands of God who can raise the dead. God can raise dead relationships, dead dreams, dead opportunities, and even dead bodies. You may not be able to see that now. Perhaps all you can see right now is the cross of your disappointment. But, a new direction, a new opportunity is waiting, if you choose to live in the hands of God.[1] Holding on to this belief is the only way to survive disappointment.

Perhaps there is no greater struggle than recognizing again and again that God's view of success and failure is different from our own. And, it is God's view, which really matters. Moses and Paul fixed their gaze upon a destination. Phillips Brooks and Barbara Brown Taylor fixed their eyes on a career. Yet, what really matters to God is whether at the end of the pilgrimage, those God calls have learned patience and humility and have entered into an utter dependence upon God. Ultimately, the destination is quite a secondary thing. It is the quality of the pilgrimage that matters. We don't have access to the private thoughts of Paul and Moses as they experienced disappointment. Nor do we have that access to Phillips Brooks or Barbara Brown Taylor. But, each placed their lives in the hands of God and trusted their future to God's care. They remind us that nothing, not even the deepest disappointment life can throw at us, can ever separate us from the love of God. Amen.

---

[1] I am grateful to Craig Barnes, President of Princeton Theological Seminary for this insight.

Are You Afraid?
Mark 4:35-41

Listen for God's Word

"Jesus asked them, 'Why are you frightened? Don't you have faith yet?'
Overcome with awe, they said to each other, 'Who then is this?
Even the wind and the sea obey him!'"
Mark 4:40, 41

That wonderful preacher, Bryant Kirkland once said, "It is fair to say that Jesus went to the cross with fear, but not anxiety."[2] Dr. Kirkland sought to make clear the difference between fear and anxiety. He states that fear is that disturbing emotion that organically affects our bodies and our outward behavior. It is the result of actual or anticipated danger or pain. Fear is a part of the human condition and to deny that Jesus experienced fear is to deny a piece of his humanity.

On the other hand, anxiety may be understood as how we deal with our fear. Do we allow our fears to become vague and, as a result, become oversized? Do we approach fear with hopelessness? If so, our fears become destructive. More importantly, anxiety is an indication that we have lost trust in anyone or anything that may come along to help us. Dr. Kirkland is correct; it is fair to say that Jesus went to the cross with fear, but not anxiety. Over and over again, Jesus surrendered himself to God in prayer and in that was his peace.

Notice in our lesson this morning from Mark's Gospel that Jesus never says, "There is nothing to be afraid of." That would be ridiculous. The storm in the story was indeed fearsome as are the "wind and waves" that threaten us. Rather, Jesus asks, "Why are you frightened? Don't you have faith yet?" Jesus is not saying that everything is going to turn out okay, though in this story it does. That is not what Jesus means by "faith." What Jesus is asking his disciples about is the quality of their relationship with God. Do they not yet have that relationship with God that gives peace in the face of fear?

This past weekend millions watched the Super Bowl. And, down to the last four seconds, millions were praying for a Raven victory. But, hear this; millions were also praying for a forty-niners victory. They could not both win though there was a mother at the game that wished exactly for that! Faith is not about one outcome or another. Faith is about trust in a relationship regardless of the outcome. Jesus took his fears to God in prayer and in the quality of that relationship with the Father, found peace rather than anxiety. Jesus overcame fear by surrendering himself to God over and over again, trusting that God would be present.

There is one area of life where many of us understand this: marriage. During a wedding ceremony, the bride and groom make promises to one another. The promises usually go something like this: "I promise to be there for you, in health and in sickness, in riches and in poverty, in joy and in sorrow." Notice, no one makes a promise for the material or physical outcome of those being married. There may be health or sickness, prosperity or struggle, joy or sorrow. The promise made is in the quality of the relationship; one will be there for the other, regardless. The faith Jesus speaks of here is the quality of the relationship between the disciples and God.

Let's return to our story this morning in Mark's Gospel. Notice how the story unfolds. The disciples become afraid of the storm that is swirling around them. Fear become anxiety and they turn to Jesus and ask, "Don't you care?" Can you imagine turning to Jesus and asking that question? I can. I have. Yet, the question speaks to the quality of the relationship with Jesus and to God. "Don't you care?" The question suggests that there is relationship work to be done.

Jesus stands up and gives orders to the wind and to the lake, "Silence! Be still!" One Bible scholar says that this is a far too tame translation of what Jesus spoke. "Muzzle yourself!" is a more accurate translation.[3] With the authority of the spoken word, the wind settled and there was a great calm. That is when Jesus asks them the faith question, the relationship question, "Don't you have faith yet?"

It seems to me that Jesus calming the storm was less about the need for the storm to stop before something terrible happens. The development of the story suggests that Jesus provided a demonstration for the disciples of the power in whom they are asked to place their trust. Jesus wants the disciples to have confidence that no matter how fierce the storms are that we face, no matter how many crises crash upon us in our journey we call life, nothing has greater power than God. The great miracle of this story is not the calming of the wind and sea. The great miracle is that a relationship with God has the capacity to calm us in the midst of a storm. As my friend Howard Edington once said, "God may not calm every storm but God will calm us in every storm." As we continually develop our relationship with God and become more conscious of God's continued presence with us, there seems to be less and less reason to be afraid of anything in life.

Ernest J. Lewis once shared this story. A young minister in Australia made a pastoral call on one of his older members. As he went into the room, he noticed a chair was pulled up by the bedside. He said to the man lying on the bed, "I see I'm not your first visitor today." The man answered weakly, "I'd like to explain that. When I was a little boy, I had difficulty praying to Jesus; so my minister suggested that when I sat down to talk to him, I pull up another chair. Then I'd talk to him just as if he were sitting right there."

The young minister left after reading the Shepherd's Psalm, the Twenty-third Psalm. A few days later, early in the morning, there was a knock at the pastor's door. An anxious daughter sobbed out her story. She told him how her father had died without her being present. "I went out of the bedroom only for a few minutes to rest. I was only gone for just a little while. When I returned he was gone. He died alone and I am so sorry for that. There was no change in him from when I left the room except for one thing. His hand was on the chair."[4]

Friends, the Christian affirmation is that we were made for fellowship with God. When we understand that, we also understand God's desire that we surrender every fear, every worry, and every concern to him in prayer. It is then that we place our hand on the chair, confident that God is there. It is how Jesus overcame fear and he invites us to the same. Amen.

---

[2] Byrant M. Kirkland, "Look Fear in the Eye," *A Pattern for Faith* (The Fifth Avenue Presbyterian Church, New York City, 1983), 159.

[3] William C. Placher, *Mark: Belief, A Theological Commentary on the Bible* (Westminster John Knox Press: Louisville, 2010), 76.

[4] Ernest J. Lewis, "A Walk Through the Valley," *Best Sermons, Volume X: 1966-1968 Protestant Edition*, edited by G. Paul Butler (New York: Trident Press, 1968), 173.

Are You Struggling with Guilt?
1 John 1:5-9

Listen for God's Word

"If we claim, 'We don't have any sin,' we deceive ourselves and the truth is not in us."
1 John 1:8

In January of 2000, I stood in the pulpit in Irving, Texas and said, "Thank you" for the privilege that had been mine for nearly six years to be the pastor of that church. That past week the membership of that church had received in the mail my resignation as their pastor. I had now accepted a call to Pennsylvania.

Following that service, a man and woman approached me and asked to join the church. I asked, "Did you hear that I am leaving as the pastor?" "Yes!" was their reply. "That is why we are ready to join!"

That is not what they really said. What they said was that they did hear that I was leaving and that they were sorry to see me go. Nonetheless, they had been visiting for several months and had fallen in love with the membership of the church. They asked again if I would receive them into membership.

When someone wishes to join a Presbyterian Church there are a few simple questions that must be asked. These questions help to determine how an individual will join. "Have both of you been baptized?" "Yes." "Are you now an active member of another church?" "No." Their answers indicated that they would join by Reaffirmation of Faith. "What's that?" they asked. It's an honest question and one that is often asked. "The first question," I responded, "is do you acknowledge your need for God's forgiveness in the person of Jesus Christ?" "No," they answered. "What?" I asked them somewhat surprised. "No, we do not need God's forgiveness." "Pastor, my wife and I love Jesus very much and are disciplined in how we live. We live in a manner that is consistent with what God asks. We simply do not disobey God."

After I caught my spiritual balance I said to them how sorry I was but that I just remembered that the next Sunday the leaders of the church received new members was the first Sunday after I had left.

Pay attention to our lesson this morning. The Bible tells us clearly, in both the Old and New Testament, that if we claim that we are innocent before God we deceive ourselves and the truth is not in us. God calls us to reach down to the bottom of the human soul, to cast a light in the dark places where our sin is hidden, so God can deal with it.

My friend, Howard Edington once said, honesty brings healing; secrets bring shame. God wants to remove our shame. That is accomplished by our honesty with God. It is not necessary to tell any other person. But, you have to be honest before God, to reach down to the hidden places of your soul and give your stories to God. God will take your stories; the stories that bring you shame, and nail them to the cross. And, God will then give you another story, a story of forgiveness and honor.

The great actor and film director Woody Allen claims to be an atheist. On one occasion he was asked the question, "If there is a God, and if that God should speak to you, what would you most want to hear him say?" Woody Allen's answer speaks for all people. He said, "If there is a God who should speak to me, I would most want to hear him say three words, 'You are forgiven.'" John says the only way you will ever hear from God the words "you are forgiven" is if you speak the words, "I have sinned."[5]

When the King of Prussia visited a Berlin prison in the 17th century all the inmates crowded around him professing their innocence. Each one claimed they had not committed the crimes for which they were imprisoned. Everyone made the same claim, everyone except one man. He remained in his cell and never spoke. The King was intrigued by that. He approached the prisoner and asked, "What are you charged with?" "Theft," answered the prisoner. "Are you guilty?" asked the King. "Yes, my Lord, I am guilty. I am receiving what I deserve." The King then turned to the guards and said, with considerable urgency, get this man out of here and release him! I don't want him contaminating all these innocent people. Well, that speaks to our teaching from John this morning, doesn't it? There is something about being honest with God that sets us free from yesterday's failures.

How does Jesus do that? Jesus takes the blame, the responsibility for our sins. Understand, someone has to take the blame and responsibility. If no one does, then it is no different than a declaration that the offense was no big deal. Make no mistake, friends. Sin is a big deal. Think about your own sin that you have tucked away from everyone. How does it make you feel? Do you need further convincing that your sins are a big deal? Sin sours our life, poisons the soul, and consumes us with darkness.

Life is diminished by our sin and we live with the weight of guilt and shame. Sin is serious because it has serious consequences upon the quality of our life. So, God takes our sin seriously. That is because God takes us seriously. God wants for us a life unfettered by guilt and shame, a life that is lived in the daylight, a life that is lived in joy. So in his Son, Jesus, God says, "I take the blame, I take the consequences, all the way to the cross where they are destroyed."

Sometime ago a historian writing for *The Atlantic* magazine suggested that June 6, 1944 is the most significant day in modern history. That was the day of the Normandy invasion where thousands of lives were lost. But, did you know, that the full responsibility for that massive invasion fell squarely upon the shoulders of General Dwight D. Eisenhower? The night before the invasion, this four-star General spent hours visiting the young soldiers under his command. He spoke to them with affection, like a father to a son: like he was speaking to each of them for the last time. Then as wave after wave of planes and boats and troops headed off into the darkness Eisenhower stood transfixed, his eyes filled with tears.

Eisenhower then returned to his quarters and with his own hand wrote a message that was to be delivered to the White House in the event the invasion failed. Of course, the invasion didn't fail so the message was never delivered to the White House. But, it did make it into history. Here is what Eisenhower wrote: "Our landings have failed. The troops, the air, the navy did all that bravery and devotion to duty could do. If any blame attaches to this event, it is mine alone."

Of all the bravery that day, this may have been the bravest of them all, argues the historian. The General took the blame before the blame needed to be taken. That is what we see in the life of Jesus. Jesus says, "I know you are going to fail. It is serious. It can darken your life forever. Come to me. I take the blame, all of it." It is, my dear friends, the only way we can ever hope to move past the guilt and shame of our brokenness and enjoy God forever. Amen.

---

[5] David L. Allen, *Preaching the Word: 1-3 John: Fellowship in God's Family*, (Wheaton, Illinois: Crossway, 2013), 31.

Are You Grieving?
1 Thessalonians 4:13-18

Listen for God's Word

> *"Brothers and sisters, we want you to know about people who have died so that you won't mourn like others who don't have any hope. Since we believe that Jesus died and rose, so we also believe that God will bring with him those who have died in Jesus. So encourage each other with these words."*
>
> 1 Thessalonians 4:13, 14, 18

Martin Luther said, "I have held many things in my hands, and lost them all; but whatever I have placed in God's hands, that I still possess."

There is a delightful story of the Englishman who was riding on a train from Scotland to London absorbed in his morning paper. Because he was reading the newspaper, he didn't notice when a very cheery Scotsman boarded the train and seated himself directly across the aisle from him. The Scotsman said to the Englishman, "Good morning." The Englishman was so absorbed in the newspaper that he didn't respond. The Scotsman then said, "Isn't this a beautiful country?" Again, the Englishman ignored the Scotsman. In one final attempt to get the Englishman's attention, the Scotsman leaned over the newspaper and said, "How do you like Scotland anyway?" Unable to ignore the Scotsman any longer, the Englishman responded, "I hate Scotland. It's cold, it's damp, and there are too many Presbyterians here." The Scotsman replied, "Well then, my friend, why don't you go to hell? It's warm, it's dry, and there are no Presbyterians there!" I invite you this morning to hear an important truth: whether we are going to London, heaven or hell, we are always moving from one place to another.

This is precisely the important truth that the Apostle Paul is making to the Church in Thessalonica; that we are always moving from one place to another until we reach our final destination of eternal life with God. Death isn't the end. Death is merely movement from life here on earth to life with God in heaven.

Yet, these words from Paul are among the most misunderstood words in the entire Bible. The misunderstanding goes something like this. If we have faith in God and believe in the promises of Jesus Christ, then when a loved one dies we will not grieve. After all, grief is for those who have no faith: for those who do not have the promises of the Bible to assure them of eternal life. Those who believe know with certainty where their loved one goes after death so we must choke back tears. That is the faithful response to the death of someone we love.

This is not what Paul is saying here in 1 Thessalonians. Paul wouldn't say this. Paul understands that grief is a part of God's most perfect design of human beings. Grief is the most natural way that we demonstrate to others and to ourselves that the one who died meant a great deal to us; that our lives are the richer because of them. No, Paul is not asking us to stand strong in the midst of loss and avoid expressions of grief. What Paul is asking us is not to grieve like those who have no hope in the person of Jesus Christ. Grieve, yes. But, grieve differently.

That, of course, begs the question, what is the difference? The difference is an important one. Those who have no hope in Jesus Christ haven't heard the Gospel; that in the power of the cross, death is destroyed and everlasting life is received. For those who haven't heard the Gospel, death is simply the end. There is no more for the person who has died. Such loss, such grief is devastating. Relationship with someone once loved is forever gone. That is how those "who don't have any hope" grieve.

Paul fully expects that we will experience grief when someone close to us dies. What Paul is asking is that we remember the promises of our faith, that death isn't the end of life. Paul is encouraging us to experience grief that is mingled with the good news that our separation from a loved one is only temporary. God's promised resurrection from the dead is for those we love and for us. Because of God, there will be a heavenly reunion for all who have died. And, at that time, death will be no more, promises the Book of Revelation. What each of us will have is life that never ends with one another and with God. That is the Gospel. That is the good news of our faith. With that knowledge, we grieve differently because we know we shall be with our loved ones again.

Please understand that the period of grief is different for each person. Some may experience grief for many years following the death of a loved one. Don't be alarmed if grief lingers for a long time. But, always hold onto the knowledge that there is more to come. The relationship that we treasured, the relationship that enriched our lives, has not come to a final end. In Jesus Christ, we shall be together again. Grief is simply an expression that what we had with another was very good.

In our lesson from Mark's Gospel, Jesus confronts a man who is out of his mind. He is so crazed that he howls day and night and cuts himself with sharp stones. Mark tells us that people have become terrified of him, that no one is able to restrain him. Yet, Jesus confronts him face to face. Jesus isn't frightened of him.

John Claypool, that wonderful preacher tells us that he had a New Testament instructor once advance a theory of why this man was so crazy, so out of his mind. The clue was in the man's location; the man was in a cemetery. According to this one biblical scholar, it may be that this man brought a loved one to the cemetery to be buried. And, he is one of those that Paul speaks of that have no hope. The man thought that death was the end: the end of life, the end of their relationship. Such was this man's despair that he literally lost his mind and was unable to leave the place where he buried his wife, his brother, or dear friend. His grief defeated him. That is until he is confronted by the person of Jesus. In Jesus, he sees for the first time the hope that there is more to life than death can take away. In Jesus Christ, hope is restored: that he will again continue the relationship that ended with death.

Paul wants us to understand that death is movement from one place to another. The power of death is destroyed when we grasp this truth of our faith.

There is something more in Paul's words to the Church in Thessalonica. Paul concludes his teaching on death and eternal life by instructing us to "encourage each other with these words." Paul's concern is that grief may become so great for any of us that we forget the promises of Jesus. The result, then, is that we fall into hopelessness and lose our minds like the crazed man in

Mark's story. As a community of faith, we are to watch out for one another, stand with one another in loss and encourage one another with the promises of our faith.

Many of you know that I have a deep admiration for great preachers, both those who lived before me and those who practice their craft today. One preacher whose work has deeply influenced my own preaching died before I began preparation for ministry, Andrew Blackwood. I was introduced to him through his written works. For some twenty-five years, he taught preaching at Princeton Theological Seminary.

Imagine, then, the sheer joy I experienced in the year 2000 when I began my ministry as pastor of Lenape Valley Presbyterian Church in New Britain, Pennsylvania and learned that a member of that congregation was one of Andrew's sons, Phil Blackwood. I developed a friendship with him that became one of my greatest treasures, personally and professionally.

Mr. Blackwood and I shared frequent lunches where he shared rich stories of growing up at Princeton. Among Mr. Blackwood's colorful stories of life in Princeton was that Dr. Albert Einstein was the baby-sitter of choice for the Blackwood family. Isn't that amazing, that Dr. Einstein enjoyed babysitting?

Some days Mr. Blackwood would put on a suit and tie simply to accompany me for a drive through Bucks County as we spoke of ministry and preaching in particular. One day I asked him if there was anything I could do special for him. He mentioned that it had been a very long time since he had been in Princeton, that he would enjoy seeing Princeton with me. We made plans for that to happen.

When the day came for our time together in Princeton, Mr. Blackwood was again in a coat and tie. We made the hour's drive to Princeton. We walked the familiar campus of Princeton Theological Seminary, stories around every corner. He showed me the home he grew up in and the home, just next door, where Dr. Einstein lived. We then walked the campus of Princeton University, which is next door to the seminary, followed by a late lunch. Following lunch, I could see that Mr. Blackwood was exhausted and I suggested that we return home for the day. There was no disagreement from him.

I walked Mr. Blackwood to his room at the retirement community where he lived and as we were saying goodbye, he said to me, "Doug, I love you. You are a good friend. I'll see you in the morning." He then repeated, "I'll see you in the morning." I had no plans to see Mr. Blackwood the next day and my schedule was already full of appointments. But, he was ninety-one years old, tired from the day at Princeton, so I just thought he was confused and said nothing.

The next morning when I arrived at work there was a man waiting for me in the parking lot of the church. He introduced himself as the nephew of Mr. Blackwood. He told me how much his uncle loved me and his gratitude for all that I had done for him. I quickly asked why he spoke in the past tense. "I am sorry," he said. "I thought you had been told. My uncle died last night in his sleep."

My tears were instant. With a man I had just met, I could not control my tears. "How? What? We were just together yesterday. He told me that he loved me. He told me..." Then I remembered. Blackwood is a Scottish name. The Blackwood family was a Scottish family. Scottish Christians have a saying they share with loved ones when they know they are dying, "I'll see you in the morning," meaning that we will see one another next in heaven. They are words meant to encourage loved ones so they will have comfort in their loss.

The Apostle Paul tells the Church in Thessalonica, and he tells us, to encourage one another so that we don't lose hope. Mr. Blackwood must have known that he was dying. His last words to me were of Christian hope. That is the other side of grief. Amen.

Are You Lonely?
Genesis 2:15-18

Listen for God's Word

"Then the Lord God said, 'It's not good that the human is alone.
I will make him a helper that is perfect for him.'"
Genesis 2:18

In 2018, Cigna, a major health insurer in the United States, paid for a national study that included the participation of physicians, psychologists, and professional therapists. What was learned is that loneliness affects more than one-third of American adults. The worst affected are young adults of 18-22 and older adults. The study concluded that loneliness is at epidemic levels in the U.S. and ranks alongside smoking and obesity as a major threat to public health. The physical effects of loneliness include inflammation, a weakened immune system, heart disease, and mental decline. Recently, the United Kingdom appointed a Minister of Loneliness to direct government resources to address loneliness.

This morning, I invite you to an examination of the Bible and what it has to say about loneliness. As early as the second chapter of the Bible, Genesis 2, God declares that, "It's not good that the human is alone. I will make him a helper that is perfect for him." In the Gospel of Mark, we learn that Jesus took steps to end his loneliness: "He appointed them to be with him."

It is important that we make a clear distinction between solitude and loneliness. Jesus sought solitude often, and so should we. Solitude is the intentional practice of being alone for the purposes of being with God: of listening to God. Loneliness is a relational condition of lacking regular, meaningful connection and fellowship with another. Solitude is important for spiritual health. Loneliness is not God's intention for us and is detrimental to our physical and emotional well-being.

As I have read and studied the Bible for thirty-one years as a pastor, I have found at least three spiritual lessons that can help us be less lonely this year. For clarity, I have named them: *A Question, A Reminder*, and *A Charge*. Each assumes an intentional response by those who may be experiencing loneliness.

A Question. The question that Jesus asks is this, "Could my loneliness be my own fault?" In the fifth chapter of John's Gospel, Jesus approaches an invalid who has been lying by the pool of Bethesda in Jerusalem for thirty-eight years. Legend was that the angels would stir the waters of the pool each day and the first person in the pool would be healed of any infirmity or illness.

Jesus approaches the man and simply asks, "Do you want to get well?" Notice that the man makes excuses for why he hasn't been healed. He blames others for "cutting in line" ahead of him and receiving the once a day healing. Jesus interrupts his "pity party" with a command, "Get up! Take your mat and walk." The crowd was astounded when the man did just that!

Jesus' question is not as insensitive as we might presume. Jesus knows that we often prefer to "lame" and "blame" in life rather than take personal responsibility for our difficulty. C. S. Lewis once commented that a familiar difficulty is frequently more desirable than an unfamiliar freedom. It takes courage to accept responsibility that you may be the one to blame for your loneliness.

A Reminder. You belong to God. You belong to Jesus. You belong to the body of Jesus, the Church. In the fifteenth chapter of John's Gospel, Jesus calls us friends. We are no longer called servants or slaves. Jesus desires to have a friendship with us.

Leslie Weatherhead tells a story of a friend who, as a little boy, adored his father. The father's work required him to be away from home for days at a time, occasionally for weeks at a time. There was always considerable anticipation for the day the father would return home. Following a two-week absence, mom and son were on tiptoe waiting to hear the father's key in the front door lock. Before the father arrived, the boy misbehaved and was sent to bed early as punishment. Well, you can send a child to bed but you can't make them sleep. That young boy lay on his bed carefully listening for the sound of his father's key in the front door. When he heard it, he leapt out of bed and ran down the stairs to the front door. He was certain he would receive further rebuke from his mother but he didn't care. His father was home. When the front door opened, the father scooped-up his young son in his arms and said, "My very own son! I love you!" That young boy, now an adult, told his friend, Leslie Weatherhead, that at that moment he was filled with an intense sense that he belonged. That is precisely what God wants each of us to experience when Jesus calls us friends.

Often times we tend to have a conversation in our minds that goes something like this: "I may not be a saint but I am not the worst person I know. I know that I get a few things wrong, but I get a lot more things right. I work hard, make an effort to please God, and I simply want what I deserve." Trust me, when it comes to God, the last thing you want is what you deserve. The good news of our faith is that God doesn't give us what we deserve. God gives us what we need and that is friendship. We belong to God as people who are deeply loved.

A Charge. God expects us to be in service to one another. In Paul's letter to the Church in Ephesus, we are reminded that each person is responsible for the ministry of the Church, not just the clergy of the local congregation. Look around for persons who may be lonely and ask them to coffee or lunch. Make yourself available to them. Invest your life in others.

Shortly after my godfather, J. R. Carmichael lost his wife, he entered a nursing home. Several months after he entered the nursing home I paid him a visit. When I inquired at the guest services center for his room number, I was told that he was never in his room. It seems that each morning Mr. Carmichael would shower, dress, eat breakfast, and then move from one residential room to another. In each room, Mr. Carmichael would talk with the resident about their family, read the Bible to them, pray with them, and conclude by telling them that he loved them. Then, it was off to the next room to do the same thing. Mr. Carmichael missed his wife every single day following her death, but he was never lonely. He took seriously God's call to invest himself in the lives of others. By his obedience, Mr. Carmichael redeemed them, and himself, from loneliness.

Some years ago, I heard the story of a young child that was lovingly tucked into bed by his parents. After his bedroom light was turned out and his parent left the room, the young boy could not sleep because of the crack of the lightning and the rumble of the thunder outside. Only minutes after his parents left his room there was a particularly scary strike of lightning, filling his room with light. He cried out and the parents rushed back to his room. They comforted their son by reminding him that God was right there in the room with him, again kissed him goodnight and left the room. Sometime later, the lightning struck again particularly loud, filling the young child's room with light. Again, the boy cried out. The parents reminded their son once again that God was with him and that he wasn't alone. The boy then said, "I know that God is here with me but I need someone with skin on them!" Don't we all.

We are called "Christians" on purpose. It literally means, "Little Christ." We are called by God to be "Christ" to one another, to be present with one another so that our physical presence may be a visual reminder of the presence of the risen Christ. As we anticipate this new year, it can be less lonely if we embrace the three lessons from this morning: Ask do I want to get well? Remember that I belong to a faith community, and that we are charged by God to look after one another and care for them. May these lessons transform this year for each of us. Amen.

Are You Forgiving?
Matthew 5:21-24

Listen for God's Word

"Therefore, if you bring your gift to the altar and there remember that your brother or sister has something against you, leave your gift at the altar and go. First make things right with your brother or sister and then come back and offer your gift."
Matthew 5:23, 24

Thomas Long once shared with me that worship depends upon a congregation of people who seek to be reconciled with each other. Damaged relationships among the people of God diminish worship. That is why Jesus teaches here in Matthew's Gospel that if your relationship is damaged with another, don't worship. There is relationship work to be done first. And, I believe there is nothing that speaks more powerfully to our need for a Savior than our human condition that seeks to hurt others when we have been hurt.

Many of you are aware that I enjoy country music. My book, *Nurture Faith: Five Minute Meditations to Strengthen Your Walk with Christ*, has about twenty meditations based upon some of my favorite country songs. Naturally, the themes that speak powerfully to me are love, longing, forgiveness, and expressed desire for a second chance. However, there is a song I cannot listen to: I Hope by Gabby Barrett. That is because it captures powerfully that part of the human condition that desires to hurt another because she has been hurt: "I hope she makes you smile. I hope you know she's the only one for you by the end of the night. And then I hope she cheats like you did on me." There is a damaged relationship. There is a damaged soul. For such a person, worship is difficult. Jesus wants more for each of us than that. So, if there is relationship work to be done, stop your worship, and go and do that first. Then return to church and complete your worship.

Relationships are damaged by one of two ways: You have hurt someone or someone has hurt you. It really is that simple. This message is limited to the latter: someone has hurt you. Jesus asks that we do relationship work by forgiving the person who has hurt you. The best place to begin is to explore what forgiveness is not.

First, forgiveness does not require reconciliation. You are the person who has been wounded. The relationship work you do to heal, to extend forgiveness to another, does not require a response. If the other person refuses your forgiveness, or dies before it is given, you are not held hostage. Forgiveness is primarily a work that we do internally. How it is received is of little importance.

Second, forgiveness does not condone the other person's action or behavior. The gift of forgiveness is the decision not to hold onto the pain any longer. It is releasing the pain and hurt so that we can move on unencumbered by what has been done to us.

Finally, forgiveness does not mean that there will be no consequences for the behavior or action of another. There may be legal consequences. We may establish parameters for a continuing relationship with that person.

What Is Forgiveness? Forgiveness is about the process of moving forward in our lives rather than the process of seeking to get even or revenge. Someone once said that holding onto anger is like drinking poison and expecting the other person to die. Forgiveness is letting go, not necessarily because the other person deserves the forgiveness, but in order for you to move forward. Without forgiveness, resentment grows and resentment is very corrosive. Your own life is diminished as a result.

There is a marvelous story of two men who belonged to a religious order that forbade any contact with women. Members of the order took vows never to physically touch or speak to a woman. One day an older, wiser member of the order took a long walk with a younger member. They journeyed for several hours into the surrounding forest. Along the way, they crossed through a small brook. Another hour or so passed and heavy rains arrived. The two turned around and began their walk back to the monastery through the rain. When they arrived back at the brook they previously crossed, it had become a mighty rush of water from the rain. A woman stood on their side of the water struggling with the need to cross. The older monk silently took the woman in his arms, carried her across the rushing water, and gently placed her down on the ground on the other side. She thanked him and went on her way. The two men then quietly walked several more hours back to the monastery.

After the two men arrived home, the younger man was strangely silent. The older man asked what was on his mind. He answered that he was deeply disturbed that his mentor could so easily break their solemn, sacred vows by carrying a woman across the rushing water. His mentor said, "I placed her down on the other side and moved on. You are still carrying her." That is precisely what we do when we refuse to forgive. We carry the greater burden.

Forgiveness is an act of generosity. Yes, it may be argued that the other hasn't asked for forgiveness nor deserves forgiveness. Yet, the generosity I speak of is not for the other person. It is an act of generosity that you give to yourself.

Michael Brown shares a story of a woman who was struggling to recover from what should have been a routine surgery. What should have been only a two-night stay in the hospital stretched on for many more nights. Her pain increased, her appetite decreased, she maintained a low-grade fever, and she had virtually no energy at all. Countless tests were run, all with negative results. One morning her surgeon, while making his rounds, sat on the edge of her bed and began to speak. "I am a good surgeon," he said. "You could've gone to any hospital in the country and not received better care than you have received here. I did my job. I removed from your body that which was making you ill. By now, you should be home, getting ready to return to work. Instead, if anything, you appear even sicker than when we admitted you." He looked her in the eyes and continued. "I did my part. I removed everything a surgeon can remove. But, I think there is something else inside you that only you can remove. And until you do, you will not be well." Thereupon he took his clipboard and exited the room.

The woman said her first inclination was to call him back and say, "How dare you speak to me that way?" However, she reported, "Instead of doing that, I simply broke into tears. I sat alone in my hospital room and wept because I knew he had guessed correctly." Many years before, the woman's husband, whom she'd loved and trusted, walked out of her life and married someone else. She had very little warning and was not given a chance to try to salvage her marriage. He simply announced that he was going and, almost that quickly, he was gone. "He was the man I thought I would grow old with," she told Michael. "He was the one I believed in, but he betrayed me. And, from that day on, I was never able to get past the anger. I simply managed it. At least, I thought I did. I believed I kept it under control, but that day in the hospital I realized that perhaps it was controlling me."

So, the woman sat in her hospital bed that afternoon and wrote a letter to her former husband and his wife. In it she wrote, "I forgive both of you and wish for you a long and happy life." The following day, her fever broke. The day after that, she was released from the hospital. One week later, she was back to work. "Perhaps," writes Michael Brown, "her ultimate step toward physical healing was something neither the surgeon nor anyone else could do for her. She embraced wellness only when she practiced forgiveness."[7]

Forgiveness is not a single act but a disposition, an attitude. We must not approach forgiveness as if it is available in a limited supply. Forgiveness is a commitment to a way of life and the manner we decide to address the wounds and pains that will inevitably come our way.

Some years ago, in Meridian, Mississippi, I volunteered in a local soup kitchen for the homeless and others who simply needed a complimentary meal at noon. As I was serving, I was made aware of someone who was standing in line along with everyone else: a local judge. When I had served everyone who had been in line, I served myself and asked the judge if I could sit with him. Naturally, I was curious about his presence at the local soup kitchen and asked him his story. Looking around the dining area, he told me he knew nearly everyone there. For one reason or another, they had appeared before him in the courtroom. After several years of handing down sentences for various minor offenses, he began to grow cynical and he didn't like who he was becoming as a result. His wife noticed. His children noticed. His friends noticed. He realized that he had to do something before his attitude toward the poor and homeless became corrosive. After considerable time in prayer about this, he sensed God calling him to get to know these people outside of the courtroom. That is when he began sharing lunch with them at least once a week. They all know him now.

He said that they still appear before him and he still has to hand down judgement for their offenses. But now, he does so with a broken heart, a softer heart. And, he continues to look for opportunities to connect them with public services to help them with long-term needs. No longer does he see the people as lazy and unlawful. He sees them as children of God who are broken and struggle to get by day after day. His whole disposition has been changed. Practicing an attitude of forgiveness accomplishes the same thing.

All this leaves the question, how do I forgive? What on earth can we do to move past the wounds we have and arrive at a place where there is healing? Permit me to share a few things I have learned from others in thirty-two years of ministry.

First, ground yourself regularly in the knowledge that God has forgiven you. In Christ, God has shown what forgiveness looks like. Romans 5 teaches that while we were sinners and not worthy, God died for us so that our sins may be forgiven.

Second, when we have been hurt, name it. Forgiveness is not trying to ignore the pain or trying to forget. That will eat you up inside. It is naming what happened to us and saying, "This is awful and this is how I feel" that permits healing to begin. That is why community and friendships are so important. We need to name our hurt to others as a starting place for moving forward.

Once we have named our hurt we then begin to look at the other person through a different lens; we begin to look at the one who hurt us as a broken person who desperately needs to experience love. Resentment, bitterness, and anger only compound the hurt that we experience. But when we begin to view the other person as someone who has also been hurt at some time in their life, as someone who also wants to be understood and loved, we empower healing for both parties to begin.

Finally, do not neglect prayer. Pray for the person who has wounded you. If praying for them is difficult in the beginning, ask someone to pray for them on your behalf. That may be the most difficult thing to do, depending upon the depth of your wound. Yet, the power of prayer can change both parties and can result in a new relationship with the other.

Each of these actions can move you from the pain of a damaged relationship to a new beginning; one free of the weight of hate and pain that diminishes our life. Amen.

---

[7] Michael Brown, *Love is the Way: Ten Steps to Discovering Personal Happiness* (BrownHouse Press, 2018), 72, 73.

Are You Hopeful?
1 Corinthians 15:1-20

Listen for God's Word

"He appeared to Cephas, then to the Twelve, and then he appeared to more than five hundred brothers and sisters at once—most of them are still alive to this day, though some have died."
1 Corinthians 15:5, 6

Some of you are aware that about two weeks ago my wife and I returned from a Caribbean cruise on the Princess Cruise Lines. On the first morning of our cruise, we met the person who would be our waiter for the entire cruise. His name was Christian. On that first morning, as he was taking our order, he took notice of the cross ring on my right hand. He complimented the ring and I said, "Yes; I am a follower of Jesus Christ. I am a Christian." I looked up at his name badge and saw that his name was Christian. Just below his name, the name of country he was from was identified: Macedonia. Now if you have ever cruised, I know many of you have, you are aware that many of the cruise lines hire people from all over the world. It is part of the richness of cruising to meet people from various countries that perhaps you will never have the opportunity to visit. And, here was a member of our wait staff that morning, Christian, who was from Macedonia.

After I identified myself as a Christian, and taking note that he was from Macedonia, I said, "The Apostle Paul went from Macedonia!" His eyes lit up and he responded, "Yes! And it's because things didn't work out for him!" "What?" I asked. "You know the story, certainly", he said. "Paul wanted to go to Bithynia and it didn't work out for him. It was closed to the Apostle Paul and he couldn't get in. He waited for God to tell him what was next in his life. And, God sent him to my country, Macedonia. I am a Christian today because God sent Paul to Macedonia." In that brief conversation, I realized the message I would preach for Easter morning.

The message is simply this. Take note of it. Write it on the blackboard of your mind. Pencil it into your worship bulletin. Remember it all this week. The message that I want you to hear this morning is the message that I believe becomes resoundingly clear to us in the Gospel of Jesus Christ. This is the message that we need not fear the failures in life. We need not fear the things we lose in life because God has a greater plan for our future. Hear it again: We need not fear the things we lose in life. Because God has a greater plan for our future!

The Apostle Paul felt a deep conviction to go to Bithynia and plant a church for Jesus Christ. It is all laid out for you in the sixteenth chapter in the Book of Acts. Wanting to be faithful to the Gospel, and wanting to be faithful to God's claim on his life, he strived to go to Bithynia and the doors never opened. So, he went back to Troas. And, when Paul went back to Troas he had two choices, the same choices that you and I have today. When something doesn't work out for you, you have two choices: You can give up. You can recline. You can despair. You can pity yourself. Or, you can keep your eyes fixed on the risen Christ and wait for God's direction for what's next in your life.

Things didn't work out for the Apostle Paul when he tried to get to Bithynia. Christian was absolutely right that morning. Rather than recline and groan and complain that life was not going in the direction that he wanted it to go, the Apostle Paul kept his eyes on the risen Christ and received a vision: A man from Macedonia came to Paul and said, "Come! Come and help us." In the tenth verse of the sixteenth chapter of Acts, Paul made immediate plans to go to Macedonia. Paul did not need to fear the lost opportunity to go into Bithynia for God had much bigger plans for Paul.

I want to take a moment and be very honest with you about my own sense of call to ministry. Five years into my ministry, that was twenty-seven years ago, for whatever reason, I felt a certain sense of call from God to serve a church in the City of New York. That call continued to grip me, and embrace me, and I became more and more convicted year after year. I wish I had the time to walk among you and lay out for you what happened in my life that made me convinced that I was to serve a congregation in New York City. Suffice it to say that I anticipated the day when that call would arrive.

Seventeen years after feeling that call to New York, while serving a congregation in Bucks County Pennsylvania, I received a phone call. The man identified himself as the chairperson of the Senior Pastor's Search Committee for the Central Presbyterian Church in Manhattan. "Dr. Hood, your name has been given to us as a possible candidate for the next Senior Pastor of our congregation. Our search committee has watched a number of your sermons on Live Stream in the past month. We would like to invite you to New York and have a conversation with us."

I shared with him that just that week, the Trustees of the church I currently was serving in Pennsylvania signed legal papers to begin construction to expand and update our church. We had begun a $1.5 million capital campaign to pay for the construction. We were renovating and expanding our church and we would be moving the congregation out of its Sanctuary, for at least six months to another space, as the Sanctuary was gutted, reimagined, and rebuilt. I said, "We are just now beginning that process. With all my heart, I cannot believe that God would ask me to leave this congregation just as we take the risk of a major expansion and renovation program." He said that he completely agreed and understood. But, he asked me to understand that they could not stop their process. The chair of the search committee had a responsibility to his own church. He had to move forward in their search for their next pastor. I thanked him for his call and continued my ministry in Bucks County.

Two years later the renovation of our plant was complete. We had a beautiful church. The Stewardship Campaign was successful. We were debt free. We had raised and collected all $1.5 million. The congregation had grown and all the staff of the church, except for the secretary, had retired or moved to other opportunities. Things were going brilliantly.

Then one day I was walking with my wife as we did each evening around George Bush Park in Doylestown, Pennsylvania. She asked me this question. "Do you sense that God has finished God's work for us here?" I said yes. It was unmistakable. God had finished what God had intended through me in Pennsylvania. So, I began the process of looking for what was next in my life. I do know that my eyes went immediately to the City of New York.

May I tell you that within the next nine months of beginning the process of looking for what was next in my life, I received an invitation from a congregation in the San Francisco Bay area, an invitation from a lovely congregation on the east coast of Florida, and an invitation from the congregation of the First Presbyterian Church of Delray Beach. Yet, I heard absolutely nothing from New York City.

May I share with you with all honesty and sincerity that I prayed one night and said, "O Lord, you raised Christ from the dead, but you do not know geography very well. The opportunities you are presenting me could not be further from the City of New York!" But, as Grace and I continued to pray about the opportunities that came our way, both Grace and I felt the strongest call that we had ever felt in our entire ministry together. God's "next" for us was at the First Presbyterian Church of Delray Beach. And, that conviction is as strong now as it was seven years ago.

New York City became my Bithynia. I wanted to go into the city, but the doors were closed. I didn't need to fear the loss of opportunities or failures in my life, because God had something much grander for my future and me. With all my heart, I believe that it is right here in Delray Beach.

Paul did not fear the things that he lost in life because he knew that God had something so much bigger for him. The question that I place in your hearts this morning is this: What is your Bithynia? What are those opportunities that you've longed for, worked for, and struggled for, that never came to fruition? Where are the failures in your own life? Where are the disappointments in your life? Those are the Bithynia's in your life.

I ask you to ponder, where is your Macedonia? Do not fear the things you've lost in life. God has a bigger plan for you. God has for you your own Macedonia. We need not fear the things that we lose in life. For God has a bigger plan for us. Naturally, for us to capture that vision and to move into God's future for us, we must keep our eyes fixed upon the presence of the risen Christ right here in the midst of our lives. We must pay attention to God's activity as Paul did in Troas so we can hear the voice calling us to Macedonia, wherever that may be.

N.T. Wright is probably one of the most prominent theologians living today. Many have called him the modern day C.S. Lewis of the Christian faith. N.T. Wright says that a strange thing happens in Christian churches on Easter morning throughout the world. We see the attendance swell. Among that large gathering of people, N.T. Wright says, will be a large number of people who are skeptical of the faith. They are skeptical of the teachings of the Christian Church. They are skeptical of the resurrection of Jesus Christ. They are in church but are present for many other reasons. Maybe it's important to their spouse. Maybe they feel it's the right thing for their children. Maybe they are making mom and dad happy. Maybe it is because they live where there continues to be a cultural expectation that Easter is for church and family dinners. But, whatever the motivation, said N.T. Wright, the Church is filled with skeptics. And, they're the people who want the Church to accept the burden of proving the resurrection of Jesus Christ before they believe. But then, Wright continues, Easter morning turns the tables on them. Rather than having the Church prove the resurrection of Jesus Christ, the tables have been turned, and now the burden is on the skeptic to prove that the resurrection didn't happen.

This is what I mean. How many of you this morning can remember what happened on September 11, 2001 in the City of New York? Please raise your hand. Wow! For those of you who were not born, I'm glad you're here. How many of you remember exactly where you were when you heard the news of 9/11 in New York? How many of you would say that your life was changed in some way because of that attack on New York nearly eighteen years ago?

Then you need to hear this: the resurrection story that I read to you from First Corinthians 15 was the first time the resurrection story was written down. It was written down before the Gospels of Matthew, Mark, Luke, and John were ever written. The first time the resurrection story was written down was right here in the fifteenth chapter of First Corinthians. And, it was written down fifteen years after the resurrection of Jesus Christ, less time than the time that has passed since the attack on New York City.

Paul says that when Jesus Christ was raised, he appeared to more than five hundred men and women at the same time. They saw Jesus

Christ, who was crucified, dead, and buried, placed in the tomb, and now is standing before them. They saw the risen Christ and they could not stop talking about it. Because they began talking about this unexpected miracle of a dead man coming back to life, the Church began to experience explosive growth. And, the Church continued to grow until today we have over three billion Christians around the world.

N.T. Wright says, the reason that the Church grew so quickly is because when this resurrection story was written down there were some five hundred people who remembered it happening and they couldn't stop talking about it and sharing with others how their life had been changed by the resurrection of Jesus Christ. N.T. Wright says if you are a skeptic then you have to prove to the Church why the resurrection didn't happen. The burden is not on the Church to prove the resurrection of Jesus Christ. The burden is on the skeptic to explain the testimony of five hundred people who, when Paul wrote it down fifteen years later, said, "Yes, this happened. It absolutely did and my life has been changed!"

Friends, we never need to fear the things that we lose in life because God has something so much bigger for us. John Ortberg, that wonderful pastor in the San Francisco Bay area, said that the people here in the fifteenth chapter of First Corinthians are experiencing something of an endless hope. What John Ortberg means to say is that these people have experienced missed opportunities, disappointments, and failures in their lives as we all do. Yet, they never gave up hope because they saw with their eyes the raised Christ in their presence. And, if God could do that, they believed that God had something so much bigger for them as well. Mark it on your minds. Write it on your worship bulletin. Remember this: that the promise of Easter is that we need not fear the things that we lose because of the living Christ who lives among us. God has something so much bigger for us. Amen.

Sermons by
Greg Rapier

Greg Rapier is the Associate Pastor of First Presbyterian Church of Delray Beach, Florida. He has degrees in English and Film, as well as a Master of Divinity from Princeton Theological Seminary, where he received The George E. Sweazey Award for Excellence in Homiletics. He is currently studying for his Doctor of Ministry degree at Pittsburgh Theological Seminary. Greg believes strongly in blurring the boundaries between the secular and the sacred, and that everyone has something valuable to contribute to the life of the Church. He lives in Lake Worth, Florida with his wife, Lissette, and their baby, Pierre.

When You Feel Inadequate
Acts 2:1-21

"In the last days, God says, I will pour out my Spirit on all people. Your sons and daughters will prophesy. Your young will see visions. Your elders will dream dreams. Even upon my servants, men and women, I will pour out my Spirit in those days, and they will prophesy."
Acts 2:17, 18

The Reverend Jan Ammon preaches maybe five times a year. She's an incredibly talented worship leader, a seasoned pastor from The Fifth Avenue Presbyterian Church in New York City. So talented that Princeton Theological Seminary hired her to organize the chapel services that run every day during the school year. A large portion of her job is partnering with the school president, professors, and students to develop liturgy and prayers to make each service feel unique. But, she doesn't preach all that often. Five times a year, maybe.

Every year she preaches on the same topic: Imposter Syndrome. So, twenty percent of her sermons or more are about Imposter Syndrome. If you are fortunate enough to be sitting in the pews of Miller Chapel during one of these sermons, you will hear from the student body, as soon as she utters the word "Imposter," a huge smattering of applause and excited gasps. The sermons are that good: the topic is that important.

So what is Imposter Syndrome? Imposter Syndrome is a psychological term describing those who are unable to internalize accomplishments and those who go about their days in constant fear of being found out, of being exposed as a fraud. The idea is that you've gotten where you are in life through luck, and deep down you know you don't really deserve what you have.

The woman who gets a big promotion assumes there weren't any other qualified candidates for the job. The high-powered executive gets nervous before a presentation because she fears her colleagues will discover her inadequacies. The man who marries the girl of his dreams believes himself to be incredibly lucky because, well, what's so special about me? If you have ever heard a young adult use the word "adult" as a verb, as in "I did some real adulting today," that's another sign of Imposter Syndrome. Because the person is implying deep down he is not an adult, but today he passed as one. Or, in the context Jan Ammon was preaching to, for the student body in Princeton, this high-pressure boilerplate, it goes something like this: I got into a really good school full of intimidatingly brilliant people, and if they only knew me, the real me, they'd know I don't belong.

Yes, Imposter Syndrome is prevalent all throughout Princeton. It's not prevalent only in Princeton. Imposter Syndrome affects over seventy percent of us. Imposter Syndrome is not limited to the professional world, the academic world, the dating world, or the adulting world; it's present in the Church too. Here, in the pews.

If we're honest with ourselves, we all have times in our journeys of faith where we feel inadequate; where we feel guilt and shame centered around not being good enough, not being Christian enough, not being faithful enough, not knowing enough. We feel like imposters.

Maybe this feeling comes to us in a moment of clarity after we've slipped up and fallen prey to our favorite sin. Or, maybe it comes at church. So often, we look at the people one or two pews over: the way they're dressed, the way they smile, the way they pick up their Bibles and effortlessly turn to the right page when reading Scripture. We look at the model-lives of church people, the Sunday morning snapshot, everyone in their Sunday best, and we compare that not to us at our best, but to our worst; to the inner turmoil that gnaws at us, to that little voice that tells us we're less than or not enough.

It goes something like this: Reading the Bible? I have a Bible at home somewhere, but I don't open it as much as I'd like to. Prayer? Yeah, I pray when I remember, but I forget more often than not. Devotionals? I mean I've purchased one or two, but I've never done any with consistency. Christian living? If only these people knew the things I've done, the life I've lived, they'd throw me out of the church.

If only they knew about my marriage, my past, the way I've driven my family away. If only they knew about my addiction, my impure thoughts, my sexual desires. If only they knew about the people I've wronged. If only they knew about my utter lack of Christian thought outside of Sunday mornings, how irrelevant God can be sometimes in my life, surely they'd kick me out of the church.

And so, we're afraid to ask it, but on some level, we do. We ask ourselves, Am I enough? Am I good enough? Am I Christian enough? Do I belong here? In church? Or, there, in heaven, with God? Am I enough?

There're two traps here with this line of thinking. One is to say, No, I'm not good enough. Everything you've said so far, Greg, is right. If people knew the things I've done, if people knew who I am deep down, they'd see me as a fraud and they'd throw me out. Or, maybe they wouldn't throw me out, but certainly, they'd think less of me. I know I'm inadequate compared to the person sitting next to me. That's one trap.

The other trap is to say you know I actually am doing pretty well. I give generously, I'm here every Sunday, I'm generally a successful person. In fact, I know I'm in better standing with God than the person sitting next to me is. That's the other trap.

So one trap is to look at yourself as a less-than Christian, and another is to go about the world looking at others as less-than Christians. This is something I'm convinced we all do, a lot of the time. It's easy and natural to sort ourselves this way: to put up these sorts of borders and to draw these boundaries. To say I'm in and you're out, or you're in and I'm out. It's easy and it's natural and it's also, really unhealthy. It's also really un-Christian.

Back when Jesus walked the earth, the temple in Jerusalem was at the center of Jewish religious life. The temple was holy. The center of the temple was known as the holy of holies. This central area was separated from the rest of the temple by a veil. This wasn't a flimsy veil either. This veil was estimated to be about sixty feet high, and early Jewish tradition says its four inches thick. On the other side of the veil, in the holy of holies, is where God was believed to dwell.

Only one person was "worthy" to enter the holy of holies: the high priest, and the high priest could only enter once a year. God was contained to one space, accessible to one person, once a year.

But then, Jesus came. And, Jesus died. And, everything changed.

The temple veil, that great structure, sixty feet high, four inches thick, ripped completely in two and things would never be the same. God escaped into the world, permanently. No longer was God only for the high priest. No longer was God only accessible for one person one day a year. No, God made God's self available to all of us, all the time. God could no longer be housed by one people or controlled by one individual. God destroyed all boundaries of religiosity and proved God's self uninterested in our classifications of who is good enough and who is not. God's work through Jesus Christ was for everyone. Jesus' death on the cross was for everyone. Everyone. EVERYONE.

Jesus died to eliminate boundaries of religiosity. Jesus died to eliminate distinctions between who's in and who's out. Jesus died to eliminate questions of "Am I good enough?", because he was good enough and he died on your behalf.

Fast-forward to Pentecost, the day we remember today, the birthday of the Church. All God's people are gathered in one place. There are Jews and non-Jews. People who would traditionally be in and people who would traditionally be out. A diverse group of people together, not unlike what we have with us today at church. And, God continues that work of tearing the curtain in two, of not being contained or confined.

On Pentecost, God erupts onto the scene. The Holy Spirit bursts into the meeting. There's flames, there's fire, there's tongues, there's red, and God speaks to everyone in their own language. God meets them where they're at, exactly as they are. God speaks to them and God works with them.

God doesn't stop them first and ask them about their job title or their qualifications. God doesn't ask them how much money they make a year. God doesn't ask them about their education. God doesn't ask them how they dress, how they smell. God doesn't ask them how old they are or what language they speak. God doesn't ask them about their race or nationality. God doesn't ask them about their level of devotion, about their past successes, or past sins. God comes to them and meets them where they're at and fills them with God's spirit. Then God says, Follow me. I have plans for you.

Many of us have heard the Pentecost story before. But remember, for the crowd gathered that day, this was not the status quo. Again, they're used to only one person, the high priest, having access to God. Here in a glorious, powerful, chaotic, frightening situation it only makes sense that some people in the crowd aren't entirely sure what's going on. What happens next in the text is Peter stands up and interprets for the crowd what exactly is happening. He quotes the Old Testament Book of Joel and says: Your sons and daughters will prophesy, your young will see visions, your elders will dream dreams. Even my servants, men and women, everyone will be arrested by the spirit of God.

Did you hear that? Your young. Your elders. Your sons. Your daughters. Your servants. Men and women.

Age doesn't matter. Gender doesn't matter. Ability doesn't matter. Race doesn't matter. How you dress doesn't matter. Whether you smile enough doesn't matter. Whether or not you arrived to church on time doesn't matter. Whether you can quote a bunch of Scripture by heart doesn't matter. Where you come from or where you've been doesn't matter. Whether you're good enough doesn't matter. All that matters is that God is good. And, God chooses you.

Now make no mistake, God will change you and hone you and develop you in ways you could never imagine. God will challenge you to do things you never thought you could. But, when it comes to God's love, there's no such thing as being not good enough. There's an old quote that goes: God loves you just as you are, but too much to leave you that way. God's going to work on you, but make no mistake: God loves you first.

There's a book my mom used to read to me that I hope one day to read to my future children. It's a little book called, *I'd Choose You.*

Parents of preschoolers, I know you have plenty of books for your little ones, but I'm telling you *I'd Choose You* is where it's at.

It's about an elephant named Norbert. He's talking to his parents about everything that went wrong that day at school. And, everything went wrong that day at school. Nobody sat with him on the bus; at lunch, he fell face first into his mashed potatoes; and he was the last person picked for baseball during recess.

Then his mom goes through every moment of Norbert's day, and she says: If I were on that bus do you know who I'd sit next to? Norbert says the name of the most popular girl in school. His mom says: No that's not it. Norbert's mom says: If I were picking teams do you know who I'd choose first? Norbert says the name of the star athlete, and his mom says: No that's not it.

The process repeats itself several times, then Norbert's mom says: If I could choose one elephant to sit next to on the bus, one elephant to be on my team, one elephant to have as my child, I'd choose you.

Norbert's done nothing to deserve his mom's love. There's nothing special about him. He's not popular, he's not athletic, and he's not particularly talented in any way. None of that matter to his mom, who repeatedly tells him: I'd choose you.

Pentecost is God choosing us, all of us, exactly as we are, without qualification. Pentecost is God saying it doesn't matter if you think you're enough, because you're enough for God.

Wherever you are today, whether you think you belong in the holy of holies or somewhere far outside the temple; whether you're far along in your spiritual journey or just beginning; whether you envy the family in the pew next to you or you think you're doing pretty well more or less; know this: you are enough for God, and God loves you just as you are.

Friends, Jan Ammon ends her Imposter Syndrome sermons at Princeton saying something like this: You were chosen for a reason. You belong in this institution, you belong in this chapel, and it is no fluke. So, friends, I end today's sermon saying the same to you:

God chooses you for a reason. You are in this house of God for a reason. God will meet you exactly where you're at and use you to do magnificent things. You belong, you are a child of God, and you are absolutely enough. Amen.

When You Feel Doubt
John 20:24-31

Listen for God's Word

"Thomas responded to Jesus, 'My Lord and my God!'
Jesus replied, 'Do you believe because you see me?
Happy are those who don't see and yet believe.'"
John 20:28, 29

You know how explaining a joke makes it less funny? You know how taking apart a joke and analyzing what makes it work seems to render lifeless whatever charm the joke had to begin with? Well, friends, I'm about to ruin a joke for you. The good news is that it's not a particularly good joke.

So, how do you keep a Baptist from drinking all your beer on a fishing trip? Invite two of them.

Now I know plenty of Christians, Baptists, Presbyterians, all varieties, good people who do not drink, many who have never even had a sip of alcohol. I am not one of them, but they absolutely exist. Anyway, the general gist of the joke, and this is where I make an unfunny joke even un-funnier, is that we religious types often do in private what we'd never admit to doing in public. Put one Baptist on a boat, and again, we're not picking on Baptists, and he'll drink with you. Put two on a boat, and neither one will drink.

Because there's just certain things we're not supposed to do, right? There are certain things we as people of faith sometimes feel bad about admitting, even if at times many of us, or even most of us, find ourselves doing it.

Doubt is kind of like that, isn't it? One of those things most of us have wrestled with, but few of us dare to name. How do you ensure that a Christian won't express any doubt? Invite two of them. Doubt is something we as Christians aren't supposed to do, something we don't like to admit that we do, and something we certainly don't want to reveal about ourselves for fear of looking bad. The truth is just about everybody doubts: Christians doubt their Christianity, atheists doubt their atheism, even agnostics, the best doubters of them all, doubt their agnosticism. Because faith, and with atheism and agnosticism, faith in nothing is faith in something, because faith and doubt are as inseparable. They're like yes and no, as heads and tails, one cannot exist without the other.

The wildly popular Netflix series *Stranger Things* is an eighties throwback sci-fi show akin to the type of movies Spielberg used to make – movies like *ET*, *Super 8*, and *The Goonies*, what I affectionately refer to as the "Kids on Bikes" genre. In each one of these movies, kids discover something bigger than them. It inevitably falls upon the kids' shoulders to go out on their bikes, undertake adventures, and restore balance to the world.

In *Stranger Things*, the kids discover something non-human has started sucking people into a realm known as the upside down. The upside down is exactly like our world, it's tethered to our world, except everything's the opposite. To describe the upside-down in the show, the kids pull out a game board, and they show how one side is decorated colorfully with little squares and movement spaces for the game, but if you were to flip that board over, you're left with nothing but black space. It's the same board, but the liveliness of the board has disappeared. The game as you know it has vanished and its shadow side is revealed. That's the upside-down.

It's the same board, the two sides are tethered together, but the two faces couldn't be more different. Where there was light, there is darkness. Where there was once good, there is evil. Where there was once joy, there is sorrow. Where there was once something there is nothing. When people from their town begin getting sucked into the upside down, it's up to the kids on bikes to pull them out.

Doubt is the upside-down of faith. It's faith's shadow side, and it's inextricably bound to faith. One side's light, the other's dark; one's full of joy, the other full of sorrow; one's hopeful and the other is hopeless. We all, each one of us, slip between these two states of being at one point or another. It's part of the game we play. The theologian Paul Tillich describes this relationship, saying, "Doubt isn't the opposite of faith, it's an element of it." They're inseparable.

To a certain level, doubt is normal. Those questions you ask yourself at night, or those questions you're too afraid to ask yourself at night, they're normal. They're part of the faith. Let's go ahead and admit to one another that there are times where our faith falters. We can admit that this isn't a Baptist-boat situation. Let's be upfront about our doubts, because at one point or another you and I have both doubted. But also at one point or another, something drew you back, here, to Jesus Christ, to the Church, something bigger and brighter and more life-giving than doubt.

Doubts will come. Doubts have come. Some of you I imagine may be doubting Jesus right now. Some of you may have doubted Jesus for a long while now.

The good news is we have for you today two passages of Scripture that address this fundamental question of what do you do when you feel yourself begin to doubt. In today's Scripture reading from John, Jesus has appeared to the other disciples, but not to Thomas. The disciples tell Thomas what they have witnessed, and Thomas doesn't believe. He expresses his doubts and is henceforth and forever known as Doubting Thomas, no wonder we don't want to admit when we have doubts. Who wants to be called, Doubting Greg or Doubting Doug?

So Thomas expresses his doubts, excuse me, Doubting Thomas expresses his doubts. He says, "Unless I see the scars in his hands and the hole in his side, I won't believe." That's the end of the scene. That's it.

If you read your Bible too quickly, you'll conflate what happens next as part of this scene but that's not how it went. We know Thomas expresses doubt and we know Jesus shows him the scars. We know Thomas is moved to belief. But, between those two passages, between the doubt and the scars, between disbelief and belief, eight days pass. Eight days of doubt. Eight days of darkness.

What is often read as one scene is actually two distinct scenes separated by eight dark days. In this first scene, Jesus is nowhere to be found, is he? It's just the disciples. The disciples tell Thomas about Jesus. Thomas tells the disciples he doesn't believe about Jesus. That's it, that's the end of the conversation. It ends in Thomas doubting, and with Jesus nowhere to be found.

Because we're now comfortable admitting when we doubt, we're also comfortable admitting that we've felt this way at one point or another, right? To feel like Jesus is nowhere to be found. You've had the thoughts. What if this isn't true? What if I've got it all wrong? What proof do I have that Jesus is risen? Where have I really seen Jesus? When we doubt, it often feels like Jesus is nowhere to be found.

When you feel distant from Jesus, when you feel Jesus is nowhere to be found, when you feel your faith fading away and doubt creeping in, remember what happens next in the story: The disciples tell Thomas about Jesus, Thomas tells the disciples he doesn't believe, end of scene. Eight days pass. Thomas is left doubting, and we are left doubting too.

Then Jesus comes bursting in. The doors are locked, but Jesus doesn't care about locked doors. He comes in anyway, greets the disciples, and then immediately turns his attention to Thomas. Poor, Doubting Thomas. He turns his attention to Thomas, and he says, "Okay, I'll show you. I'll show you my scars, but in order for you to see them and in order for you to feel them, I need you to take me by the hand. Place your fingers here."

Thomas does as instructed, Doubting Thomas trusts in Jesus enough; Doubting Thomas has faith enough to take Jesus by the hand. Isn't that ironic, doubting Thomas has faith in Jesus, and when he takes Jesus by the hand, he feels the scars and realizes whose hand it is he holds.

Friends, the risen Lord Jesus Christ went after Thomas. He burst in through a locked door, and he went after Thomas. He came to Thomas in all his disbelief, he reached out his arm, he asked Thomas to take him by the hand, and he invited Thomas to come and see; see what he had done.

The same is true for each one of us. When you doubt, you'd better believe the risen Lord would come after you, not with fire and brimstone, but with open palms and wounded hands. The risen Lord will come after you and show you his scars. He will show you his hands. And if you have the faith to take Jesus by the hand, that's it, just that much faith, if you have the same amount of faith as Doubting Thomas, you too will find yourself saying the words of Thomas in the Scripture, "my Lord and my God."

Today's other Scripture can be found at the end of Matthew's Gospel. The Scripture is known as the great commission, Jesus' final words to his followers, words of instruction and words of encouragement: Go forth and make disciples of all nations, baptizing them in the name of the Father and the Son and the Holy Ghost, and remember I am with you until the end of the age.

Most of the time when we hear this passage, we think about what it is Jesus calls us to do, we think about the essence of what it means to be a follower of Jesus, and rightfully so, that's what the passage is about.

What strikes me currently is the stuff around Jesus words, the very beginning and the very end of this section. The Scripture says, "When the disciples saw Jesus they worshipped him, but some doubted." That's the line we get before Jesus' big speech, but some doubted.

What does Jesus do with the doubters? Well, the exact same thing he does with the rest of his disciples. He appears to them. He proclaims to them good news. He calls them to participate with him in making disciples of all nations. Friends, Jesus appears to the doubters, loves the doubters, speaks to the doubters, and equips the doubters. Jesus calls the doubters to work alongside the rest of his disciples: therefore, Jesus calls his disciples to work alongside the doubters. Whether you are a believer or a doubter or a sometimes-believer, or a sometimes-doubter, Jesus will appear to you, care for you, and call you to work together with others for something bigger than yourself. That's the promise Jesus makes here.

That's beginning of this passage: but some doubted. I told you I'm also interested in the end, Jesus' final words to his disciples. Jesus' final words to his believers, to his non-believers, to his not-yet believers, to his almost believers, to his used-to-be believers, and to his maybe-someday believers. Jesus final words. Here they are, the ending of Matthew's Gospel: "And remember I am with you until the end of the age."

I am with you until the end of the age. I am with you, loyal and faithful Christian. I am with you, person who doubts. I am with you, loyal and faithful Christian who sometimes doubts. I am with you when the world is right-side up, and I am with you when you feel stuck in the upside-down. I am with you. See my scars. Take my hand. And, remember, I am with you until the end of the age. Amen.

When You Feel Alone
Romans 12:10-15

Listen for God's Word

> *"Love each other like the members of your family. Be the best at showing honor to each other."*
> Romans 12:10

When Lissette and I visit Sacramento, we normally try to squeeze in as much time together with people as possible. We're intentional about keeping contact with old friends. Between old friends, family, neighbors, and people from our old church, each visit to Sacramento has a long itinerary of people to see. We're pretty social.

About a year ago, an old friend of mine from high school, Alex, had a birthday celebration that just so happened to align with our travel dates. The city recently allowed beer trolley tours, and if you haven't seen them, these tours allow guests to sit on what is essentially a mobile bar. Each mobile bar is staffed by two people, a driver/tour guide and a bartender. The guests sit there in rows on the back of the trolley, facing each other, pedaling.

The party was an interesting high school reunion of sorts because there were about ten of us there. Out of those ten, there were about six people I hadn't seen or spoken to since I graduated back in 2009. It was cool to see how everyone's evolved. One of my classmates was now a chef. Another worked as a financial planner. Another was a bartender. And, another was finishing school to become a medical assistant.

Out of everyone there, I definitely received the most questions about my vocation. It's not every day you find out your friend is a pastor. And, it's not every day you see a pastor on the back of a beer trolley. You can drink? Yes, but I won't be drinking too much. You're married now? Yes, in fact many denominations allow their clergy to marry. What's a denomination? And, so it went.

While most people were interested in my work, there was one person I was most interested in, a man I've known since my freshman year of high school. I wouldn't say I was great friends with him, but we played football together, and I knew him. In fact, everyone in the school knew him. We'll call him Will.

Back when I was in high school, iPods were all the rage. At any given time walking the hallways, about half the school would have their headphones in. Some students had the bulky, original iPod that held thousands of songs, and others had the tiny Shuffle, but most students had either the discreet iPod Nano or the midsize iPod Video.

Not me. I had the Zune, Microsoft's short-lived, self-proclaimed iPod killer. The Zune is the butt of a lot of jokes now, but to this day, I swear to you it was a better product. I loved my Zune, until one day during PE, my gym locker was broken into and my Zune was stolen from me. There was someone I thought stole my Zune, but I wasn't going to make any accusations. I talked to a friend of mine who was connected with the person I suspected. I asked him to help me out, and he did. Sure enough, my suspicion was confirmed.

It was Will who took my Zune. As I said, everyone in the school knew Will. Everyone in the school knew Will because, as the rumor went, Will was a Crip. As in a gang member. Even I knew it might not be wise to tell on a Crip. From then on, my Zune was no longer mine. It belonged to Will.

Here we are, ten years later, seated directly across from one another, he a well-known gang member, me a pastor in the Presbyterian Church. The night went on and finally I got the courage to ask him, "you know Will, back in high school everyone always said oh, don't mess with Will, Will's a Crip, be careful around Will." I hesitated for a moment and I said, "Just out of curiosity, what's up with that? Why'd you join?"

He took a sip of his beer, and he looked at me sideways; like he was assessing me, like a long time had passed since someone had the verve, or the stupidity, to ask him that. For a moment, I was scared.

He took another sip, and finally he said, "You know Greg, the thing about the Crips people don't understand is they're like a family. Sometimes you just need someone who has your back."

While our pressures may be different from those of Will, my guess is many of us need that. Family. Someone to have our backs. After all, don't you ever feel alone in your brokenness? Like you can really use someone in your corner? Don't you sometimes feel like your situation is utterly helpless? Like your heart is chained to the floor? Don't you sometimes feel confined, condemned, to repeat the same mistakes, or to feel the same sadness? Don't you ever feel stuck in the mud of life with no way out? Don't you ever feel alone, and what you need is someone to have your back?

What struck me was that Will, who wasn't really a Christian, found family and protection and meaning in life not from the Church, but from a gang. Will, like many of us, felt a deep brokenness and helplessness; he felt confined, condemned, held captive in the mud of life. He needed someone who had his back. Only instead of joining a church, he joined a gang.

Now why is that? Maybe because that gang was more of a Church for Will than church ever was. The gang offered him meaning and family and protection, and it was present for him in a way the Church simply was not. That got me thinking about why people join gangs, about that need for family, for someone who simply has your back. That got me thinking that we, the Church, on good days, we're like a gang in that respect, aren't we? We're like a family.

Of course, that's a limited metaphor; we're not exactly like a gang. Whereas gangs spread violence, the Church spreads love. While gangs often tear communities apart, the Church seeks to bridge us together. While a gang would kill for you, the Church celebrates a Christ who died for you. There are major differences.

In one primary aspect, the Church is absolutely like a gang, and that is because we are indeed a family. We are, as a Church, a group of people who, first and foremost, we worship God. Also, we're a family who has one another's backs. It's what we are called to do.

It's a hallmark of the Church. We are to care for one another just as God cares for us. We are to love our God with all our heart and all our soul and all our mind, and we are to love our neighbor as ourselves. Or, like today's passage from Romans says: We are to love each other like family. We're to be happy with those who are happy, and cry with those who are crying.

This is both a comfort and a call. It's a comfort because as we face difficult times, we can remember that we are not alone. As we feel lonely and isolated, helpless, held captive by our circumstances, stuck in the mud of life, we can remember that God comes into our lives to release us from those circumstances that weigh us down and pull us apart.

Friends, in the fourth chapter of Luke's Gospel, Jesus proclaims that he came to liberate the captives and set free the oppressed. Sometimes that's us. God came to free us. To liberate us. It's a comfort because it reminds us we have a God. And, therefore a Church who has our back, who will fight for us, advocate for us, liberate us, and that never in life do we travel alone.

It's a comfort, but it's also a call. It's a call for each one of us to be the body of Christ. It's a call for us to be family for one another. So the question we all have to ask ourselves is this: As a member of God's family, am I pulling my weight around the house? Am I treating others as family? Am I caring for my brothers and sisters? Or, am I simply locked in my bedroom all alone with the TV on? In other words: Do I really love my neighbor as myself? Or, is all that just lip service?

The body of Christ has one another's backs in a way that a gang never could. I see it every day. Good work done by good people. I go on a hospital visit and discover other members of the church already there. I hear laughter amongst friends at youth group. I see the various ministries supported by this church and others. I see the imprint of these ministries throughout the world. I've seen the way you serve together in the community. I've seen brothers and sisters in Christ come alongside people experiencing great loss. I've been part of a great many Christian celebrations. The body of Christ really is like a family.

The Fast and Furious movies are by no means Christian, but one of the things they do get right, so much that it's become a bit of a joke, is the sense of family. One of the theses of this series is that your family is the people you choose. In *Fast Five*, which, for those of you keeping track at home, is the fifth movie of the series, Vin Diesel's character Dominic Toretto gathers everyone from the four previous movies together in a warehouse. They come from all over the world: the computer expert from Miami who debuted in *2 Fast 2 Furious*, the former LAPD officer we first met in the first movie, the precision driver from Japan, the female Israeli soldier from the fourth movie. And, an eclectic group of six or seven others gather in the room too. This is Dom's family.

They're there in the warehouse to do a job, make some money. You know how it goes in the movies. Before getting to business, Dom gives a speech where he tells his crew, "The money will come and go. We all know that. The most important thing in life will always be the people in this room. Right here. Right now." Then he raises a glass and offers a toast, "to family."

Dom's family is big, and growing, and inclusive. It includes people who don't always look like him and don't always think like him. The people in that room. That's his family.

Brothers and sisters in Christ, I hope you know that you are amongst family. That though you feel sometimes helpless and captive in your sins; that although you at times feel alienated, isolated, and lonely, know that wherever you walk, you do not walk alone. Brothers and sisters in Christ, I hope you know that you are surrounded by people who love you, care for you, who pray for you, and who fundamentally have your back. The people in this room. Right here. Right now.

Dominic Toretto in that speech gets one thing wrong, though. The Crips do too. Sometimes we as a Church forget it also. Family is not just the people in this room. If we look only at the people who look like us or think like us, we're missing the point. God's family is so much larger than that. God's family cannot be defined by any walls or geographic boundaries. It can't be defined by blood or skin or what colors you wear or your political affiliation or economic status or common interests. Because, you know this, we are all God's children.

The same Christ who tore the temple curtain in two and exploded out into the world; the Christ who met the Samaritan woman at the well and who sent us forth to make disciples of all nations; the Christ who came to proclaim good news to the poor and release to the prisoners and who demands that we love our neighbors as ourselves; the God who took on human bone and flesh, who promises that one day every tongue will gather together in praise of God's name; the God who invites us all to the great banquet of communion and who holds the whole world in those hands, that God calls us to be part of a large and vibrant and extended family. To be happy with those who are happy, and to cry with those who are crying. To put love first. To share with the poor. To fight for justice. To promote equality.

Can you imagine what the world would look like if we all took that call seriously? Can you imagine what your life would look like if you took that call seriously? How the world would transform into a better place. How your life may transform into a better place. And, how people like my friend, Will, would grow up knowing for certain that a whole army of God's people have his back. Let it be so for Will, and for you, and also for me. Amen.

When You Feel Ugly
Jeremiah 1:4-10

Listen for God's Word

"Before I created you in the womb I knew you."'
Jeremiah 1:5a

Meryl Streep is widely considered to be the best actress who ever lived. She has a record twenty-one Academy Award acting nominations, achieving a level of excellence at her craft nobody has come close to matching. She swallows every scene she's in. She wouldn't know it though, because she doesn't watch her own movies. Johnny Depp is the same way. He too can't stand watching himself onscreen. It's quite common for actors to be totally unable to watch their own performances.

Actor Jessie Eisenberg describes the experience akin to looking through vacation photographs. He describes a scenario where you've taken a hundred vacation photographs, and you really like two of them, so you use them everywhere. You send them to friends, post them on Facebook, and use them in that year's Christmas card. But, you still have ninety-eight photographs left that, in Eisenberg's words, "You're totally mortified of." Eisenberg recalls, "The side of your face, the speedo you decided to wear, that's the experience for me. You take those ninety-eight pictures and project them on a massive scale onto something that people not only watch, but critique." You get the idea.

Perhaps Reese Wetherspoon explains the feeling most succinctly. The actress says watching herself act makes her spiral into a state of self-hate. "Who feels good looking at themselves?" she asked once during an interview. She answered her question by saying, "Nobody, right?"

If Reese Witherspoon and Johnny Depp can't look themselves in the mirror, what does that mean for the rest of us? These are Hollywood's biggest and brightest stars. Individuals who have achieved a level of personal success and physical beauty which most of us can only dream. If they have a complicated relationship with themselves, then how are we supposed to feel?

Conventional wisdom says we don't feel all that well, not really. There's a reason the self-help section at the bookstore keeps growing. There's a reason mental health counseling and therapy is finally, and thankfully, becoming destigmatized, and therapy is now used openly by a growing percentage of the population. We often don't feel all that well, and we need all the help we can get.

Studies show the longer we look in the mirror, the less likely we are to like what we see. There's a lovely thought. So as you look in the mirror, you begin by recognizing, 'yep, that's me,' then the longer you look, the more you notice all your little imperfections and the gradual changes in your body, the dark circles under your eyes, that mark on your skin, is that new? Like Moses when he sees God on Mount Sinai, if you stare at the mirror too long you may start glowing.

Of course, it's not just the mirror. We listen to our voicemail and ask ourselves, "Do I really sound like that?" We say the wrong words in a social interaction only to replay our mistakes internally for hours on end, berating ourselves for not doing better. That's just the superficial stuff. We haven't gotten yet to the sin, to the ugliness we all harbor within and try our best not to think about; the endless list of ways we've let others and ourselves down. There's a lot about all of us that's hard to like. Maybe it shouldn't be that surprising that Reese Wetherspoon, Johnny Depp, and Meryl Streep can't look at themselves. Maybe there's no escaping self-doubt. Maybe that nagging inner-critic can't be turned off. Maybe that's part of being human, of being broken, this complicated self-image.

I want you to take a moment and check in with yourself. How are you feeling today? How do you feel about yourself? What's your relationship like with your body? With who you are, fundamentally as a person? What are you proud of? What is it that keeps you up at night? What are your current struggles?

In Jeremiah chapter one, the prophet makes plain his own struggles: he says he's too young, and he doesn't like the way he talks. God has asked Jeremiah to be a prophet, to be God's mouthpiece and to speak God's word to the people. Jeremiah is afraid God's got the wrong guy. Then Jeremiah lays bare his imperfections. He says, "I'm too young for this, God, and I don't speak all that good."

Listen to how God responds. God gently touches Jeremiah's lips. God looks at the young Jeremiah the way a parent looks at a child. God looks at him tenderly and with pride. God tells Jeremiah not to fear or to doubt. God declares God's with Jeremiah, and God always has been. "Even before you were born," God says, "I was there forming you in the womb, looking at you, watching, lovingly watching. I didn't look away then, and I won't look away now."

We may see brokenness the longer we look at ourselves, but when God looks at us, God sees something else. God sees beauty. God sees God's own reflection within each one of us. God sees dignity and value, someone worthy of loving and being loved. God sees someone fearfully and wonderfully made.

In Jeremiah 1:5, we hear the famous line: before I created you in the womb, I knew you, and before you were born, I consecrated you. There's a beautiful echo of that line in Psalm 139. Only in Psalm 139, the word is knit. "You knit me together in the womb," the psalmist says. "You created my innermost parts. I give thanks to you that I was marvelously set apart." You can hear God's claim upon Jeremiah echoed here for each of us. God lovingly, and carefully, and thoughtfully knitting each of us together.

We have a God who knits. It's an image reflecting a startling amount of intimacy. The God who created the universe and everything in it, the God who created something from nothing, the God who dreamt up snow-capped mountains and arid deserts, the God who looks over the whole world, this all-powerful, all-knowing, vast being took the time to personally knit you together in the womb. To know you and to see you. To stitch you together, and to bless you.

We often think of God the Father, right? That's one way we've thought about God for centuries, Father, Son, Holy Spirit. That's one way we wrap our heads around who God is. In our Scriptures, there's also a rich tradition, it's less pronounced but it's there, of Scripture using motherly language to describe God.

In the beginning, Genesis 1:27, God creates humanity in God's own image, male and female, revealing an essence in all of us reflecting the image of God, regardless of gender. There are also a few examples in Isaiah of motherly language describing God, my favorite being in Isaiah 49, where God compares God's self to a mother nursing her young. In Matthew 23 and again in Luke 13, Jesus describes God as a mother hen who protects her flock by nestling them safely under her wing.

Here, in today's texts from Jeremiah and the Psalms, God appears almost grandmotherly. Before I knit you together, I knew you. You can picture it, can't you? God sitting there in a rocking chair by the fire. God covered with a patchwork quilt, sipping on some tea, working her hands together night after night, to carefully and beautifully create you. And me. And everybody else. Can you feel the intimacy? The motherly warmth? The way God cares for each one of us?

Often we treat ourselves with coldness and bitterness. Here's an image of a God who treats us with warmth and compassion. Often our inner dialogue beats us down. Here's an image of a God who lifts us up. Often we struggle with self-hate, but here's an image of a God who loves us perfectly.

In the late nineties, sociologist Arthur Aron posited that he could make strangers fall in love. He claimed only to need ninety-four minutes, thirty-six questions, and two willing participants. Here's what he did: he had two strangers who had never met enter his laboratory through two separate doors. They sat in chairs facing each other, and they were instructed to verbally answer a questionnaire featuring thirty-six questions. The questions would start innocent enough but over time become more probing and personal. The volunteers had ninety minutes to complete the task, alternating between speaking and listening. Then, when the ninety minutes were up, Arthur Aron had the two participants look at each other directly in the eyes for four consecutive minutes without looking away or saying anything.

That was it, the entirety of the experiment. Six months after the experiment concluded, Aron's two participants were married. Arthur Aron and his entire lab were invited to the wedding ceremony.

Back in 2015, a journalist by the name of Mandy Len Catron, curious about Arthur Aron's study, decided to try it for herself. Mandy invited to the bar an acquaintance from the gym. This outing was their first time out together, and they went through Arthur's thirty-six questions. By the time they finished, it was late, and the bar was loud, so they moved to a quiet little bridge down the street to complete the experiment with four minutes of direct eye contact.

Here's what Mandy Len Catron had to say about those four minutes: "The real crux of the moment was not just that I was really seeing someone ... but that I was seeing someone really seeing me."

There's a fragility and a vulnerability in those four minutes, a tenderness, looking into this man's eyes, she could see her own eyes, and behind her eyes, she could see her own brokenness and beauty reflected in him. I like to think she also saw the image of God there in him behind his eyes; the image of God reflected back to her, just as she bore the image of God for him. I like to think she was reminded, through the eyes of a stranger, of the inherent beauty she holds within; the beauty that maybe she forgot about a long time ago.

A cold October night in a bar, two relative strangers fell in love because they took the time to notice one another, and now they too are married. Their story was published in the *New York Times*.

To know and be known, to see and be seen. That's what this experiment was all about, and that's what these couples were able to achieve. There's a beauty and intimacy to fully knowing and seeing another human being, to accessing the world through the eyes of another.

Friends, we too can see the world through eyes of another. By spending time with God, by praying and talking and listening and studying God's word, we too can see the world through God's eyes, just as God sees the world through ours. Just as God dwells with us, lives with us, and looks at us, so too can we look back at God and see the world through God's eyes. Through God's eyes, we can see this world in all its brokenness and all its beauty. Through God's eyes, we can see the inherent beauty and dignity of all God's people. Through God's eyes, we can look at people from all nationalities, genders, religions, everything, and we can see an essence that can never be taken away; the image of God reflected in them. Through God's eyes, we can see the craftsmanship of all people, and we can witness within every person we meet, someone knitted together with care. If only we look through God's eyes, we'll see.

Maybe, just maybe, the next time we look in the mirror, we'll see ourselves through God's eyes too. Loved. Fearfully and wonderfully made. Knit together in the womb. Let it be so for me and also for you. Amen.

When You Feel Like Crying
Psalm 30:5

Listen for God's Word

"His anger lasts for only a second, but his favor lasts a lifetime.
Weeping may stay all night, but by morning, joy!"
Psalm 30:5

Hagar, the servant, the slave, knows what it means to struggle. She's a woman without a voice, stuck in a life of subservience, seemingly destined for heartbreak after heartbreak. Hagar knows Abraham in the biblical sense, in the way that leads to children. If you read the Scripture, it appears Hagar has no say in it. Abraham's wife Sarah can't conceive, so she suggests Abraham go find "that Egyptian-slave-girl" Hagar and have a baby through her. We never do hear from Hagar on the matter, because as long as Abraham and Sarah are in the story, Hagar doesn't act. She's only acted upon. Hagar isn't the subject of her own sentences. She's a prisoner in her own life.

Eventually Sarah does conceive and so she has no need for that Egyptian-slave-girl Hagar or Hagar's son Ishmael. Hagar and her son are sent away. Into the wilderness. The desert. All alone. Just Hagar, her son, some bread, and a little water. Eventually she runs out of bread, and then she runs out of water. She's hot, she's hungry, she's thirsty, she's alone, and she's scared. She does what any of us would do in that situation. She cries. She steps away from her baby boy because she doesn't want him to hear her, because she can't bear to watch him die of starvation, and she just weeps.

If anyone deserves a good cry, it's Hagar, don't you think? If anyone has earned the right to cry, surely it's this abandoned, voiceless, hungry, thirsty, scared Egyptian-slave girl.

Do you ever feel like Hagar? Of course you do. Sadness is a part of life, isn't it? While my gut reaction is to couch the sadness by saying our situations aren't as bad as Hagar's, that's not really true, is it? Our pressures are just as dire as Hagar's. We, as the body of Christ, know all too well the horrors Hagar faced. Not all of us in every way, but each one of us in one way or another: we know what it means to cry. We've been hungry. We've been thirsty. We've been unsure where our next meal would come from. We've worried for our health and for the health of our loved ones. We've known people we'd rather not know. We've been silenced, scared, lonely, lost, and abandoned. We've felt trapped, prisoners to the circumstances of our own lives.

We have bills that keep piling up, tests to take, an endless stream of work, doctor visits, and funerals, so many funerals. We face rejection, addiction, isolation, degradation, and depression. Yes, sometimes we do feel like crying. On this road of life, sadness is at times unescapable and tears are not optional.

There's something that is optional though: a choice we can all make. Each one of us, even when we're overcome with sadness. That choice is to live life with joy. Not happiness, but joy. They're different. Happiness is a feeling, it's an emotion, it's fickle, here one day, but gone the next. Joy, on the other hand, is a choice; it's a conscious decision. It's a state of being in the world, of living out your life as if your life is worth living, because it is. It's a lens for seeing beauty in God's creation, even when God's creation isn't giving you much beauty to see. Happiness crumbles when faced with adversity, but joy stands tall and defiant.

The theologian Willie James Jennings describes joy as resistance to despair. He says despair seeks to make death the final word, but joy will have none of it. Joy stands defiant to death and despair and sadness. Joy says: death, you do not get the final say. Jennings says joy is a willingness to hold onto life, to spin something positive out of pain and suffering. Not that the pain and suffering was positive. Rather joy seeks to rewrite the story so that something positive will come from our sorrows. Joy is a choice, a state of being, and in the midst of sadness, joy is an act of resistance and defiance.

Friends, as we go through our lives, we will at times, each one of us, face a deep sadness. Some of us are in the midst of a deep sadness right now. When you are sad, cling to what you know is true. When you're so sad you don't know if it's true anymore, cling to what you have known to be true: that we have a God whose goodness overcomes all that is evil. A God who promises one day every tear will dry, that one day there will be no more death or mourning or crying or pain. A God who loves us totally and unconditionally and whose amazing grace covers us all. When you have a God like that, you can't help but for joy to bubble up, even when the night is dark.

The psalmist captures this dichotomy between sadness and joy. Psalm 30, verse five reads: Weeping may linger for the night, but joy comes with the morning.

Friends, there's two parts to this sentence. Most people want to rush immediately to joy in the morning, but the psalmist recognizes there is a time and a place to be sad. It's okay to be sad. Please hear that. God enters into sadness and God feels sad too. Scripture is filled with stories of God being sad. There's a space for weeping. It lingers through the night.

But it's all temporal, its impermanent. All of it. No matter how overwhelming and crushing, no matter how debilitating and dark the night feels, when dawn breaks, and dawn will break, when dawn breaks, God's steadfast love and hope and goodness will reign supreme. When dawn breaks and our tears dry, every single one of us will feel not sorrow, but joy!

Fred Rogers, the ordained Presbyterian minister/TV host was known not to shy away from difficult topics on *Mr. Rogers' Neighborhood*. In one episode, he talked candidly and openly about divorce, or, as he put it that your parents might someday decide not to live together anymore. In another, he addressed the topic of death, talking with little four-and-five-year-olds about what happens when your pet dies. These are topics other children's shows wouldn't dare address.

Our instinct when we see a child in physical or emotional pain is to reach out and make things better, right? Right? I hope that's what your instinct is! We want to fill them with joy and happiness. We want to restore their childlike innocence. We want to rush them along to "joy comes in the morning". But, Mr. Rogers with his sweaters and puppets and his television program, gave children a place to weep. To be sad. Mr. Rogers sat with children in their pain. It was only after tending to their sadness and sitting with them that he offered a word of hope. He looked at those kids through the TV screen and said, "The very same people who are sad sometimes are the very same people who are glad sometimes."

Weeping may linger for the night but joy comes with the morning. Mr. Rogers reminded children of just that.

A few years ago, as fires ravaged much of northern California, the city of Paradise, a city both Lissette and I spent meaningful time in, faced total destruction. Over ninety percent of the city's residents left for good due to the Camp Fire. Eleven thousand homes burnt down, along with most of the cities other buildings, including the local high school.

A girls' volleyball team from that high school were among the many who had to evacuate with nothing more than the clothes on their back. This volleyball team had tasted great success. They were scheduled for their semifinal championship game just days after the evacuation. They had no uniforms, no shoes, no volleyballs, no nets, no equipment, and for some of them, no homes. They decided to show up anyway. They decided to play.

They drove to the city of Auburn, about two hours south. When they arrived at the gym, they discovered something incredible. The girls of Forest Lake Christian High School, the opponents of this team from Paradise, had waiting for the girls from Paradise, brand new uniforms. And socks. And kneepads. And gift cards. And clothing. And clothing for their families. And a banquet of warm, homemade food.

Weeping may linger for the night but joy comes with the morning, and today the city of Paradise continues to rebuild.

Hagar, the servant, the slave, is alone in the desert wilderness with her child Ishmael. She has no food, no drink, and seemingly no hope. She can't bear to see her child die, so she turns away and she closes her eyes, and she weeps.

In the second half of that story, God hears Hagar's cry. God hears the cries of her child. God opens Hagar's eyes and reveals to her a

95

well of fresh, cold water right there in front of her just waiting to be used. Don't be afraid, God says. I've heard the tears of your child and I have heard your tears for your child, and he will be okay. In fact, he will be more than okay, for I am with him. He cries now, but I will build a great nation out of him.

Weeping may linger for the night but joy comes with the morning.

There's a true story about a young girl, about thirteen years old, nine months pregnant, clearly unplanned. Contrary to the expertise of medical professionals, at nine months pregnant, she decided to go on a trip. There she was on her trip, in a busy metropolitan city with people walking all around, passing by her because she's pregnant and she's slow. Then, right there in the middle of this strange and foreign city, she felt the baby start to come. Can you imagine the panic in this thirteen-year-old girl stuck in an unknown place as she desperately waddled to the local hotels, all of them, only to discover there was no room for her at the inn? Alone in a manger. You better believe this young Mary thought about crying.

Weeping may linger for the night but joy comes with the morning.

Mary's boy Jesus grew up to be a man. Now in his thirties, Jesus encountered a different Mary whose brother Lazarus just died. A crowd was gathered there with Mary and her sister Martha. They were grieving. Mary saw Jesus and said "Lord, if you had been here, my brother wouldn't have died."

Then Mary completely broke down and cried. The whole crowd around her was crying too. Even Jesus. Jesus wept, right there alongside her, Jesus wept. Then Jesus Christ, Lord of heaven and earth, proclaimed with a loud voice, "Lazarus, come out!" His tomb was opened and the dead man walked once again.

Weeping may linger for the night, but joy comes with the morning.

Not long after raising Lazarus, Jesus found himself a prisoner of the Roman state. He was spat on. Kicked. Beaten with a stick. Mocked. Whipped. Stripped. He was forced to carry his own cross, only he couldn't do it.

Then they put the cross there on the hill and crucified him. They drove stakes through his palms and his feet, and they watched him die. He didn't even last very long up there. It was a quick death, as far as crucifixions go. Some ending for the King of the Jews. It was a night full of weeping indeed.

In the morning, three days later, Jesus, defiantly, triumphantly, and joyfully rose again. Defeating death, once and for all. Defeating death, darkness, tears, sin, and evil, defeating all the dark powers of this world.

Weeping may linger for the night, but joy will rise up in the morning.

Friends, when you feel like crying, remember that a new day will come. Remember that you have a God who knows what it means to suffer, who cries with you in the night, and who will rise with you in the morning when all your weeping will turn into joy. Amen.

When You Feel Angry
Ephesians 4:26-32

Listen for God's Word

> *"Be angry without sinning."*
> Ephesians 4:26a

We all have an image of what a Christian should be. If you were to picture in your head the ideal Christian, the perfect Christian, you'd probably picture someone who wakes up early and reads their Scriptures, someone who has a dynamic prayer life, and someone who goes to church regularly. If I were to ask you to describe their general demeanor, the way they carry about themselves, I think you would describe someone like this: Someone patient. Someone kind. Someone meek. Someone mild. Someone gentle. Someone calm. A sensitive type of person. If I were to go into each one of your homes and ask you to describe your ideal Christian, I imagine very few of you would say, "You know Greg, I guess I'd look for someone who's really angry… When people shout and yell, I just feel so affirmed in my faith."

We have this image of what an ideal Christian is supposed to be, and there's no place within that image for anger. You may remember the story of Rachael Denhollander, the former gymnast for the US National Olympic Team. Rachael achieved great success in her sport, but life wasn't always rosy for her. In fact, parts of it were rather bleak. More than a decade after participating on the team, she came forward and revealed that her trainer had been abusing her.

Rachael was at first confused. Later, when she realized the severity of what had happened, she was angry. Rachael didn't know what to do with that anger, so she came forward and brought it to her most beloved and cherished community. She brought it to her church. Rachael quickly discovered that her fellow Christians ignored her hurt and her anger altogether, and they jumped instead, and immediately, to forgiveness. When reflecting upon her experience seeking help from the church, Rachael said, "It is with deep regret that I say the church is one of the worst places to go for help."

Again, we Christians can do forgiveness very well. But anger? Not so much. We don't like anger. We don't know how to deal with anger. So what happens then, to people like Rachael, when our Christianity has no room for anger? What happens to people like us? After all, just about all of us get pretty angry sometimes. What happens when all we talk about is forgiveness, but we make no room for anger?

To answer this, let us turn our attention to Ephesians 4. This passage contains verses which I am sure have been used by those seeking not to hear Rachael, but to fix her. Beginning on verse 31: "Put aside all bitterness, losing your temper, anger, shouting, and slander, along with every other evil. Be kind, compassionate, and forgiving to each other, in the same way God forgave you in Christ."

Friends, there is no way around it; this Scripture is true. We are to forgive one another in the same way God forgives us. This is part of what we all are called to do as Christians. However, this truth, these verses, cannot be taken out of context, for you cannot simply read verses 31-32 without also including Ephesians 4:26. The topic sentence of this section, the words through which we interpret everything that follows, Scripture's thesis statement regarding anger, Scripture's commandment regarding anger, four words: Be angry without sinning.

Be angry without sinning. Be angry. Don't sin, but be angry. Our Scriptures expect that we'll get angry sometimes. In fact, Scripture even commands it! Through these four words, *be angry without sinning,* we can understand all it means to manage anger as a Christian, and we can set aside that outdated and quite frankly damaging model that seeks to repress all anger. The *just don't be angry* rule is not only impractical, but it's also unbiblical. To be angry without sinning means simply this: We Christians ought to feel angry sometimes. But also, if we're not careful, we can let that anger consume us.

Scripture gives us permission to be angry. It also gives us a warning. Our understanding of anger isn't complete until we are able to hold God's permission and God's warning in communion with one another.

Let's begin with God's permission. As is the case for all aspects of our humanity, Jesus models for us what it means to be angry. In Matthew's Gospel, Jesus enters a synagogue and discovers people using the house of God for all sorts of nefarious purposes. They have tables set up, selling all sorts of currency and doves, things having no place within the temple. So Jesus gets angry. He comes in and flips the tables on their heads, not metaphorically but physically, as in Jesus Christ, the one who says turn the other cheek and blessed are the meek, the lamb of God, goes into the temple, walks up to the tables where the merchants sit and flips them over in rage and disgust.

This is what God does with God's anger, and this is what we are called to do as well. When God sees injustice happening in the world, God cannot help but get angry. When God sees God's beloved people suffering, injuring one another, exploiting one another, God can't help but get angry. You also see this played out in those scary Old Testament passages speaking about the wrath of God. The wrath of God is anger, but it's rooted in love. It's anger, but it comes from a profound sense of justice. It's righteous anger.

When you get hurt, you have every right to be angry. When someone you love gets hurt, you have every right to be angry. God loves all of us, and God calls all of us to love one another. When any one of us gets hurt, you have a right to be angry. When children go to bed hungry, you have a right to be angry. When sin and brokenness have destroyed your household, you have a right to be angry. When a virus snatches away your job, you have a right to be angry. When you lose the opportunity to go to prom and graduate with your class, you have a right to be angry. When you've been abused, you have a right to be angry. When your community of faith speaks only of forgiveness without acknowledging your pain, you have a right to be angry. When you make 81 cents for every dollar a man makes in the same position, you have a right to be angry. When you can't even go jogging because of the color of your skin, you have a right to be angry. This sort of anger is the outcry of a soul that says, "This is not how things are supposed to be." This sort of anger is a lament, it's a prayer, and it's a call to justice.

What sort of injustices cause you to get angry? What are the things in this world that break your heart and make you say *this is not how things are supposed to be?* What about in your personal life? Think about the things that make you angry, and ask yourself, *does this anger come from a place of love and justice?* Then ask yourself, and ask God, *how does my faith impact what I do with this anger? Am I being called simply to forgive? Or, am I being called to flip some tables?*

God gives us permission to be angry, but that permission is coupled with a warning. God gives us permission to experience righteous anger. God-ordained anger. God warns against a second type of anger, one I really don't have a fancy name for, so I'm going to call it what it is: bad anger.

You and I both know bad anger far too well. This is the type of anger we as Christians are often warned against. If Ephesians four says be angry and do not sin, then bad anger is anger that leads to sin. If Ephesians four says, do not lose your temper, then bad anger is anger that causes you to lose your temper and to lash out at others. If Ephesians four says, be kind, compassionate, and forgiving to each other, then bad anger has no room for kindness, compassion, or forgiveness. Bad anger is the type of anger that leads to hurt feelings and to shouting and to tears and to regret. It's shouting at a spouse or friend over something trivial. It's using less-than-Christian gestures on the freeway. It's injuring someone else out of spite. It's using your hands instead of your words. It's anger that seeks to break rather than mend. It's anger that leads to more anger.

I've been bad angry before and it is not a very fun place to be. My guess is it wouldn't be very difficult for you to think back to your own bad anger and to your own regrets. As you think back to your own bad anger, you may realize how hard it is in the moment to distinguish between anger that is righteous and anger that is bad. Because in the moment, bad anger feels like righteous anger. Sometimes bad anger is righteous anger, only taken too far. It's righteous anger that leads to unrighteous action.

Friends, anger is like fire. It can be used for great good, it can warm a house, it can cook a meal, but left unattended and uncontained it can destroy everything in its path. When you're dealing with anger, you're playing with fire. This is why Scripture gives us permission coupled with a warning, be angry and do not sin, because God knows that anger left unchecked can set lives ablaze.

There's an episode in the Children's television show *Daniel Tiger's Neighborhood* where our main character Daniel Tiger is planning a beach day. He gathers his towel, his sunscreen, and his pail and shovel. Then he finds his beach chair and his umbrella. Only when he opens the front door to leave, he discovers a thunderstorm brewing outside his doorstep. His beach day is ruined.

Daniel Tiger gets frustrated and angry, and rightfully so. He's so angry he looks as if he's about to do something he'll later regret. His righteous anger looks as if it's about to turn to bad anger.

His mother steps in. She sees his anger and places a hand on him and tells him, "Daniel, it's okay to be angry." Then she teaches him, and also the kids watching the show, a simple song: *When you feel so mad that you want to roar, take a deep breath and count to four. One. Two. Three. Four.*

Daniel Tiger's mom knows it's okay to experience anger. She invites him to experience his anger fully, but also to breathe and to control his anger rather than let his anger control him.

So when you feel angry, take a breath. Walk carefully. Walk faithfully. Righteously. Prayerfully. Practice humility. But also practice justice.

Consider again Rachael Denhollander, the Olympic gymnast who was abused by her trainer. She was angry, and she was hurt. She turned to her church and found little help there. Something within her said no, this isn't right, this is not how things are supposed to be. Instead, she turned to Scripture. She faithfully and prayerfully studied God's word and God's call upon her heart. She found within Scripture God standing up for her when no one else would, and she found within those pages God giving her permission to practice righteous anger. She spoke publicly out against her abuser. After doing so, more than a hundred fifty other gymnasts followed suit. With her righteous anger, with her faith, she spoke out, and she testified. Her testimony can be found in full online and it is a masterwork in Christian theology; I do not use that term lightly. Here's some of what she had to say, these words directed at her former trainer: *Should you ever reach the point of truly facing what you have done, the guilt will be crushing. And that is what makes the Gospel of Christ so sweet. Because it extends grace and hope and mercy where none should be found. And it will be there for you. I pray you experience the soul crushing weight of guilt so you may someday experience true repentance and true forgiveness from God, which you need far more than forgiveness from me, though I extend that to you as well.*

Yes, Rachael did do what her church originally suggested. She did offer him forgiveness after all. But, she did something else too. She sought to see him convicted. She fought for justice.

And, she was angry. Amen.

When You Feel Glad
1 Thessalonians 5:16-21

Listen for God's Word

"Don't brush off Spirit-inspired messages,
but examine everything carefully and hang on to what is good."
1 Thessalonians 5:20, 21

How do we know we've had an encounter with God? That's the question I'm wrestling with this morning. In a world where God rarely speaks audibly, especially recently in a world where the headlines on the news lead us to question God's whereabouts, where a growing percentage of the population doesn't even believe in God, and where those of us who do believe in God do so in a passive way where we really don't see God as an active agent in our lives, where we just live our lives and shoehorn God in where we can, where is God?

To make it more personal, where do you see God? How do you know when you've had an encounter with the divine?

To answer that question, we're going to begin today's sermon with two godless stories. Not godless in the sense that they're morally bankrupt, but rather godless in the sense that neither story really appears to be about God. The first story from my own life, the second from Scripture. Yes, a Godless story from Scripture.

Godless story number one: it was the night before my wedding, about 11:30 p.m., I should have been asleep, but, of course, I wasn't because it was the night before my wedding. I received a text from my friend, Shane, and her boyfriend, Jesse. They were driving to In-N-Out Burger, because that's what you do when you live in California. They had miraculously guessed that I was unable to sleep this night before my wedding. Though it was borderline irresponsible when I should be sleeping, they asked if I wanted to join them.

Naturally, I said yes. Thirty minutes later, there I was sitting in the back of their car in a well-lit parking lot on what, as of a few minutes ago, was officially my wedding day. I ate a cheeseburger and fries. We talked about how I wasn't nervous, but excited, and about how I wasn't going to be seeing Lissette again until the wedding itself when she was to walk down the aisle. I told them this whole In-N-Out situation was so weird, I'd probably end up using it in a sermon someday, but I just wasn't sure how. There was something about that moment, something I couldn't articulate that felt oddly poignant. A moment of stillness before everything was going to change.

The next morning, two of my groomsmen took me out to breakfast. I was still full from the In-N-Out, so I ordered something small like toast. If I were smarter, I would have had something more substantial, because Lissette and I were so busy during the wedding we forgot to eat! We had our breakfast, then I lingered around the house for a bit and gradually made my way to the church to get ready. When I arrived, Lissette was already there. She and her bridesmaids had been getting ready in a room in the far side of the church, and even then, we were practicing social distancing. It was all very carefully choreographed so our paths didn't cross.

Then came time for the service. I remember standing there with my pastor outside the Sanctuary door, just waiting to go in. I was excited and all sorts of nervous. I processed in. As the groomsmen and bridesmaids processed in, the organist messed up. He was supposed to play a soft little Bruno Mars number on the piano but instead he played Canon in D, which was going to be Lissette's song. Lissette ended up walking down the aisle to Bruno Mars. Let me tell you, as soon as those Sanctuary doors reopened and I saw my future wife, I did not care what song was playing. I thought she would be the one struggling to keep things together. When I first saw her, it took all the strength I could muster to fight back my tears. It was a flood of emotion. To this day, when I perform a wedding and everyone is standing for the bride, I sneak a glance to my side, because I like to see the groom see the bride.

Godless story number two: This one's from Scripture. The Jewish Esther marries a powerful king who does not know she is Jewish.

She's not the king's only wife, so they don't interact the way we think of when we think of a modern couple. Remember, this is way back in the day, and Esther's a woman, so she's very subservient to her husband, let alone her king. Even speaking out of turn could get her killed.

The king's chief minister, Haman, had come up with a plot to massacre all the Jews in the empire. With the persuasion of Esther's cousin, Mordechai, Esther decides to confront her king to tell him about Haman's plot and try to stop it, even though it could mean death for her.

Then, in a scene with so much tension it feels ripped straight from a Quentin Tarantino movie, Esther, the king, and Haman share a meal together at a banquet table. Haman wants Esther and her people killed, Esther wants to see Haman killed. More than that, she wants to save her life and the lives of her people. Unbeknownst to Haman, Esther plans on telling the king as much during this meal. If this goes well, she'll have saved her people. If this goes poorly, she'll end up dead by night's end.

"What do you want?" the king asks. Esther looks at the king, then Haman, then back at the king. Finally, she says, "I am a Jew. This man, your most trusted advisor, wants to kill me and my people. What do I want? I want to live."

The king deliberates, and eventually he rules in Esther's favor. He sends Haman to be killed, and all the Jews throughout the land rejoice and feast. The feast of Purim is celebrated by Jews to this day.

Here's the thing, and this is why Esther is literally a godless story, in the entire Book of Esther, ten chapters, God is never mentioned. Not once. There are actually two Books in the Bible that don't mention God. The other is Song of Songs, your go-to source for biblical erotic love poetry. Look it up. Or don't.

My question is this: Why do our Scriptures have entire books that don't mention God? What do these godless stories tell us about God's presence in our lives and in the world?

If our lives seem godless in that we live our lives without burning bushes speaking to us and without seas parting miraculously; if our lives are godless in that we've never walked on water or witnessed someone rise from the dead; if our lives are godless in that we can live our whole lives without thinking of or discussing God; and if the Book of Esther is godless in the sense that God is never discussed, never thought of, never mentioned, then maybe there's an overlap between the Book of Esther and our lives.

Maybe, and just humor me here, this is an outlandish claim, maybe Esther is in the Bible for a reason. Crazy, I know. I hope they don't revoke my degree for that one. Maybe Esther is in the Bible for a reason. Maybe God is there in Esther, not on the page but between the lines. Maybe, if we can unlock that, if we can find God in Esther, we can also find God in our lives. Maybe the Book of Esther wasn't godless all along. Maybe our lives aren't godless either.

First Thessalonians chapter five connects *God's will* with *everything that is good.* The Scripture says, *rejoice always, (be glad always), because that is God's will…Examine everything carefully and hang onto what is good.*

In other words, hang onto what is good because that is God's will. Because God's will is good, we are to rejoice.

I want to take a moment to clarify we often think about God's will completely wrong. When someone dies and we say *oh, God wanted another angel,* or if we experience a hardship in our lives, and we say *God-willing, I'll get through it,* I get the sentiment, but we're actually shortchanging God. God wants us to get through it. God wills us to get through it. God promises that one way or another we will get through it. God's will is that we all experience wholeness in this life and the next. God doesn't will us to suffer and to die and to experience pain. What sort of parent wants that for their child? Not a very good one, I'll tell you that much.

God is good. Our Scriptures are very clear, so let me repeat that again, God is good. All the time, God is good. God's will is good. God wills for good to happen, not bad. God is good. *Literally.* I don't mean literally the way my generation uses the term literally, I mean *Literally, God is good. God equals good.*

When First Thessalonians tells us to examine everything carefully and hang onto what is good, it's telling us to hang onto God. It's also telling us where to find God. Because God is present in the good. Friends, where there is good there is God, and where there is God, there is good. First John tells us that God is love. Again, literally, God is love. God equals love. Where there is love there is God, and where there is God there is love.

Now, friends, we have two guideposts for finding God, don't we? Where there is good, there is God. That's guidepost number one. Guidepost number two: where there is love, there is God.

In the Book of Esther, where do we see love? Where do we see good? Finding God is as simple as that. God is present in Mortacai's love and his sense of justice, as he lovingly urges his niece Esther to do what is good. God is present in Esther's courageous call to do what is right at that dinner table, where Esther is afraid to do what is good, but knows that she must. God is there in the king's heart as the king lovingly listens to his wife when she speaks something brash, and when he rules in her favor anyway. Finally, God is with the Jewish people in their gladness and in their joy as they partake in the Purim feast, for something good had happened, and that was God's will.

Friends, we can use these same guideposts to find God in our lives. Where we see love, we see God. And, where we see good, we see God.

There was something fundamentally good, irresponsible maybe, but good, about my friends taking me to In-N-Out burger the night before my wedding when I couldn't sleep. It's hard to put into words the same way God's sometimes hard to put into words. As I ate a cheeseburger at midnight in a harshly lit parking lot, I experienced something good, and I felt loved. I felt happy. I felt God.

I felt God the next morning as I shared breakfast with my groomsmen. I felt God there waiting in the church with my good and loving friends. And then, when that silly Bruno Mars song played on the organ, when finally, at the peak of a long day, I saw my bride, as I felt an outpouring of joy and of love and of gladness, you better believe I felt the presence of God.

What about you? Where are the places in your life you've encountered love? What makes you happy? What has made you feel the most alive lately? When have you felt glad? Where have you experienced good? Because that friends, is where you've experienced God.

When you feel glad, know that you are feeling something else too, God with you and in you. When you feel alive, know that that is God's will for you to experience life in all its glory. When you feel love, and feel loved, and see love acted out in the world, know that you are bearing witness to the very essence of God. Amen.

Sermons by
John C. Randolph

John "Skip" Randolph is a practicing attorney who has had a long time interest in theology and a passion for preaching. He has taken courses in theology at Columbia Theological Seminary and has received a Certificate in Spiritual Formation from that institution. Skip is an ordained Elder in the Presbyterian Church. He is married and has three children and seven grandchildren.

Searching for God Beyond the Clouds
Exodus 19:16-21

Listen for God's Word

> *"Mount Sinai was all in smoke because the Lord had come down on it with lightning."*
> Exodus 19:18a

When our granddaughter, Marion, was just three years old she asked her mother where God was. Her mother paused a bit, then responded, "God is up above in the sky watching over us." Who knows what thoughts were going through Marion's mind as she pondered the answer to her question? It became obvious she had been thinking about it, as a few days later when traveling with her mother in the car, she proclaimed from her car seat as she gazed toward the heavens, "Mommy, I can't see God. There are too many clouds."

I was delighted that our granddaughter, at the young age of three, was beginning to search for the presence of God in her life. Little did she know that she was about to embark on a lifelong search. A search that she would share with others of us who, like explorers, travel along paths, known and unknown, in our attempt to discover the breadth and depth of God's presence in our lives.

Now, were you to have asked Marion how old she was she would have told you she is "free." Not three, but free. The word "free" described Marion much better than the number three, which defined only her chronological age. At her then tender and innocent age, Marion was indeed free. Free and unimpeded to search for God beyond the clouds, clouds which in moments would clear to reveal in her mind's eye a kindly old man who would protect her from harm. At three years old, Marion was free from thoughts of other clouds that often get in our way when we seek God. Marion was free from thoughts of what dangers might lurk outside the protection of her mother's and father's arms; free from thoughts of why a person's skin color may make a difference in the way they live; free from thoughts of what a war in a far off land can mean and what it can mean in the lives of those families that war touches on all sides of the conflagration; free from thoughts of how disease and injury can snatch away life as we know it; free from thoughts of the heartbreak of lost love; free from the pain of loneliness. Marion did not know of these kinds of clouds and I prayed to the utmost depth of my being that she would be protected from these vicissitudes of life. We know of these kinds of clouds, don't we, each of us here? These are the clouds that often make us look into the heavens and proclaim as Marion did; "I cannot see God; there are too many clouds." Despite the clouds, or perhaps because of the clouds, we continue to search for God. We search for God beyond the clouds.

Our search is not an easy one. Nor was it easy for those who came before us. The ancient Hebrews were continually searching for the God they could not see. We need only turn to the book of Psalms which, through its poetry, characterizes this search. I believe the reason that many of us love the Psalms is that they define for us the base from which we live our lives today in our search for God. They define the periods of our lives in which we come the closest to God. They are three distinct periods, the first of which is the period of wonder and awe, which causes us to give praise to God, such as in Psalm 9 in which we can hear ourselves praising God as a result of our joy. "I will talk about all your wonderful acts. I will celebrate and rejoice I you; I will sing praise to your name, Most High."

Then, there are those periods of our lives in which we suffer and which cause us to cry aloud to God, sometimes cursing God and wondering about God's presence, such as in Psalm 10 where the ancient Hebrews cry: "Why do you stand so far away, Lord, hiding yourself in troubling times?" Or Psalm 13: "How long will you forget me, Lord? Forever? How long will you hide your face from me? How long will I be left to my own wits, agony filling my heart? Daily?"

And, finally, our lives are composed of periods of thanksgiving when God has lifted us from the depths of despair and we can cry out in our thanks, such as in Psalm 18: "I love you, Lord, my strength. The Lord is my solid rock, my fortress, my rescuer. In my distress I cry out to the Lord; I called to my God for help. You lifted me high above my adversaries. That's why I thank you, Lord, in the presence of the nations. That's why I sing praises to your name."

Sound familiar? Can you identify these periods in your life? Walter Brueggemann, one of the foremost and well-respected contemporary Old Testament scholars, has redefined the division of the Psalms from Psalms of praise, lamentations, and thanksgiving, to periods that he calls orientation, disorientation, and new orientation. I find this to be a fascinating concept and one that helps me define my life and my search for God.

Periods of orientation are those periods in our lives when everything is going well; periods of normalcy, periods of awe, periods of happiness in which we have reason to give God praise. Periods of disorientation, on the other hand, are those periods in which normalcy disappears, when our world falls apart, periods when we doubt God or turn from God. Periods of lamentation. Then, according to Walter Brueggemann, comes the opportunity for a period of new orientation. New orientation is something entirely different from going from a disorientated state back to a state of orientation. It is rather a state in which we learn that going back to a state of orientation is no longer good enough. Rather we must, as a result of our suffering or our disorientation, move on to a state of newness, a state in which we allow ourselves to let ourselves go to a point that we allow ourselves to truly discover God. A state we might call "new life."

I firmly believe that if we truly expect to find God in our search we must ultimately seek a state of new orientation in our lives.

Let me use September 11, 2001, as an example. Normalcy sank for all of us as we observed the twin towers of New York City's World Trade Center crumble, as if in slow motion, to a pile of rubble carrying with it the lives of men, women, and children who minutes before were carrying on with their routine activities, the same as you and me. Ask my friend Tom Tewell what happened after that. Tom was serving as the Senior Pastor at the Fifth Avenue Presbyterian Church in New York when hundreds of people began coming into the church seeking out God in the midst of this chaos. Tom Tewell was there as people sat together with dazed looks on their faces, just wanting to be there with others to try to understand, to sing together, to worship together, to weep together, and to search for God together. He was there as rich and poor, black and white, young and old came together united in their grief and in their loss. He was there as scores of adults asked to be baptized in the name of Jesus Christ. I don't know where you were but no matter, wherever we were, and we all remember where we were at that precise moment, we all observed similar results from this tragedy; people of all faiths, colors, persuasions, economic status, and backgrounds coming together. We saw American flags flapping from Ford pickup trucks and Cadillac El Dorados; from semis to Saturns; from motor scooters to Mercedes. Even the politicians in Washington couldn't find anything negative to say about each other. Church attendance increased dramatically. We felt closer to God. Then we drifted back, back to a period of orientation, right back to where we were before. Flags were found torn, tattered, and strewn on the side of the highway. Lapel pins we wore to declare our allegiance to our country were left in the bureau drawer. Church attendance fell off and our search for God became less intense. We began to cloak ourselves in our previous circle of friends and criticism of others soon became more rampant than ever before. The clouds, which had previously been in the way of our ability to see God, soon reappeared. Clouds of greed, clouds of consumerism, clouds of bigotry, clouds of hatred.

I am reminded of a story I once heard about a town in which the people who lived therein lived in houses without windows. The houses were closed up like sealed boxes. People could never look out and see their neighbors. There were no roads and the town was filled with weeds, deep holes, and huge rocks. One day the people decided to come out of their homes in search of God. They climbed to the tops of tall mountains. They traveled far into the ocean. They traveled to the desert and finally returned, not having found God. Having come out from their houses and seen their condition, the people who lived in the town started to work together. They helped put windows in the rooms of their homes, they cut the weeds, filled the holes and cleared the rocks, and they built a road between their houses. When their work was done, the townspeople gathered close together and listened as the setting sun blushed the sky a deep red. It was only then that they realized that God was right there among them. God says when you look for me, when you look out your windows, when you show concern for your neighbor, you will find me. Cut down the weeds that divide you from others. Build bridges to repair the breach. Push away the rocks. Fill the holes.

Hunter Coleman, formerly the Senior Pastor at the First Presbyterian Church in Highlands, North Carolina, once described in a prayer what he termed as the invisible God, the God for whom we search beyond the clouds, beyond the chaos of our lives. He spoke of the beauty of the giant hemlock and how its needles quiver in the wind. The wind is not seen, but we see the quivering of the needles. So too, when we see hand reaching out to hand, people walking down the halls of the hospitals and nursing homes to visit the sick and the lonely, of people helping those less fortunate than themselves, we do not see God but we see the quivering of humankind and we know God is at work.

Because God remains invisible, we continue our search. Because God is a mystery, we mortals try as we may to unravel that mystery. We try to find God beyond the clouds, beyond those things that divert our attention from our search and beyond those dark clouds that so often bring us down.

Acclaimed preacher, teacher, lecturer and author, Barbara Brown Taylor, wrote a book called *When God is Silent*. In this book, Barbara speaks of the disappearance of God and how "after Sinai, God's face was hidden from men." "Gradually," she said, "the prophetic experience of God became one of visions and dreams." "The world," she said, "was no longer a place where seas split and snakes talked, but one in which human relationship to the divine was largely a matter of personal belief." "This," she said, "is the world into which Jesus was born – the clearest revelation of God's presence on earth since Sinai. In Jesus, God was once again made both audible and visible."

Because of Jesus, although our search for God has not been made easy, it has been made less difficult. In Jesus, we see God come to life. In Jesus, we see the way we should live our lives and in Jesus, we see our hope for a life everlasting. In Jesus, we see new life, the new orientation spoken of by Walter Brueggemann to which we should devote our efforts after periods of disorientation in our own lives.

I meet with a group of men each Thursday morning. This group ranges from age 60 to age 90. The purpose of our meeting is to explore the role of God in our lives. Usually, after discussing politics, world events, golf, and other matters of interest, we get around to asking questions about God. It is a safe place. No question is considered inappropriate in our group of men because we are all there to learn and to benefit from each other. None of us has all the answers and we know that, but it helps us to inquire, to search, to pray, and to discover. We ask fundamental questions such as, who or what is God? Where is God? When do we feel closest to God? What about heaven? What will it be like? Will we meet our loved ones there? What about our enemies? Some of us are further along in our inquiries and with our answers than others. We have been doing this long enough to be able to see each other mature in our thoughts and our beliefs. I have experienced the pleasure of seeing one of our members who questioned his faith most become the most comfortable in his faith as a result of the inquiries he made as a result of our search together. Our search for God.

There are times, aren't there, when all of us have questions and when there seem to be no answers. When huge loss threatens us or swallows us up. When we are in a corner and can't get out. Or, when we are at the bottom of a pit of disappointment, despair, and even destruction. Many of us, like the psalmist, at one time or another, cry out to God at the top of our lungs. We go looking for God, seeking God, reaching up to God to ask for help.

As I spoke to our granddaughter Marion, at the young age of three, I speak also to you today. Marion, I am delighted that you are searching for God. You are about to travel down a long road, a road which will allow you to explore not only that road but all the paths to which it leads. As you travel, continue your search for God. I must tell you my dear Marion, there will often be clouds along the way, clouds that may impede you in your search for God and which may cause you to cry out years from now, perhaps when your mommy is not there to protect you, "Mommy, I cannot see God, there are too many clouds." Know this Marion, God lives beyond the clouds. Even on those days when you cannot see God because there are too many clouds, God will be there for you. God always knows how to find you Marion, and if you listen very closely, you will hear God say, "Here I am. Here I am." Amen.

Ripples and Rainbows
Genesis 9:12-17

Listen for God's Word

"I have set my rainbow in the clouds,
and it will be the sign of the covenant between me and the earth."
Genesis 9:13 (NIV)

One of the first things they taught us in law school in our trial practice course was to never ask a question in trial to which you do not know the answer. You don't want to be surprised at trial. That is why so much time goes into trial preparation and why we take depositions of witnesses prior to trial so we know exactly what witnesses are going to say and how they will answer our questions.

In seminary, in the course on sermon preparation, there are also rules. Although I never took the course, I am advised that there is a basic rule to be followed in preparing a sermon and that is to never decide in advance what message you would like to convey and then research Scripture to support your message, but to do the direct opposite. That is to go to Scripture first, do what is called an exegesis, a critical explanation or interpretation of the text, and to let your message evolve from that interpretation.

Perhaps because I never took that course, I am a bit of a maverick in the way I prepare a sermon. I usually have a particular message I want to convey and I always find Scripture supportive of that message. Today, I have gone a step further. For today's sermon I came up first with the title to my sermon and have allowed the text to follow my title, a totally unorthodox way to prepare a sermon or in fact any story or literary work. Most commonly, one writes the story and the title follows.

In this instance, however, I was inspired by a set of circumstances which lead to the title of my sermon, Ripples and Rainbows, thinking my story would flow simply and easily from that point.

A few weeks ago, I visited my brother on the west coast of Florida. We are very close, but we seldom get together. The last time I had seen my brother and his wife was a few weeks earlier in Michigan at his daughter's funeral, a celebration of a life well lived but cut too short. His daughter leaving behind a husband, two children, a brother and sister, extended family and grieving parents, who suffered a grief too hard to bear. My brother's wife suffers from severe Alzheimer's disease and my brother is her primary caretaker. Needless to say, he is not in a good state of mind. Our visit, at the time was therefore important and timely.

After visiting with my brother for some time, my wife and I went by ourselves in the early morning, to the community pool in the neighborhood in which my brother and his wife reside. It was a very quiet time of day. No one else was present. The pool was flat calm, a rain having just subsided. I was in a very contemplative mood, reflecting on the plight of my brother and his family. I sat on a lounge chair as I watched my wife step slowly into the pool. As she took her first step, I noticed ripples take shape in the pool, and without any further activity on her part, the tiny ripples began to flow, ever so gracefully, from where my wife had placed her foot to the far extension of the pool, then bouncing back to the place where she had stepped. Nothing remarkable in and of itself, but remember I was in a contemplative mood. So, when my wife and I got up to leave and observed one of the most vivid, colorful, and beautiful rainbows either of us had ever seen, I contemplated what all of this meant, what message was being conveyed to me. From that, I was inspired to come up with the title for today's sermon, Ripples and Rainbows. From that title, I thought, my message would fall into place.

But, I met with frustration on my very first try when I researched where and how many times the word ripple appeared in the Bible. Guess what I found? Zero. The word ripple appears nowhere in Scripture. The closest I came was in Psalm 147:15, which states in my Revised Standard Version; "He sends forth his command to the earth; His word runs swiftly." In continuing my research, I finally found a translation of Psalm 147:15 I had been seeking, which states, "God's command ripples across the earth. His word runs out on swift feet." (The Voice Translation) That was a start, albeit a rather weak start, in finding Scripture to support the title to my sermon. All was not lost because I knew for a fact that I would find Scripture about rainbows in the Bible. That I did, in Genesis 9:13 after the flood when God said, "I have set my rainbow in the clouds and it will be a sign of the covenant between me and the earth." I was getting closer. But, what about the effect of those ripples? What about the ripple effect?

A friend of mine, Scott Whitaker, who leads a Bible study by teleconference every Tuesday morning, tells this story. It is a story about a lady, just retired, who never was able to marry, had no children, all due to having to care for her mother most of her life. Her mother has now died, and she is all alone.

The one additional joy in her life in which she found some fulfillment and which she looked forward to each week, singing in the church choir, has now also been taken from her, as she was asked to leave the choir because she couldn't carry a tune.

So there she found herself all alone, forgotten, feeling insignificant, living in a tiny one-bedroom apartment, four stories above street level in a rundown area of a big unnoticing city; living only on her social security and what very few memories remained.

Things probably couldn't get worse, until one day a longhaired, tattooed, pierced in various parts of his face, disheveled, tough-looking young man with chains hanging off his belt, moved into that low-rent housing building. The neighbors, concerned, began to talk about being even more unsafe now. What if others like him begin to move in; they're all the same, worthless, always up to no good. Her neighbors put extra locks on their doors and she did too. Fear set in.

This went on for a while. Then one night, she was coming back later than usual from a weekday evening church service, trying to find another church where she felt accepted, worthy, significant, a place where she could make a difference.

As she entered the darkened lobby and began to climb the stairs to her apartment, she noticed that man, the new tenant everyone was afraid of, lurking in the dark shadows under the staircase. She wanted to scream out as she continued to climb the stairs. Instead, she reached down into her first love, and began to sing, "When you walk through a storm, hold your head up high, and don't be afraid of the dark." She wasn't even sure if the words were right, still trembling as she continued to climb.

"At the end of the storm there's a golden sky, and the sweet silver song of a lark. Walk on through the wind, walk on through the rain, though your dreams be tossed and blown. Walk on, walk on with hope in your heart and you'll never walk alone. You'll never walk alone." By then she had reached her apartment, went in and locked the door, grateful she was safe in her refuge from the rest of the world.

When she awoke the next morning, she found a note on a torn piece of paper under her door. As she began to read it, she realized the note was from the young man everyone seemed to fear. "I don't even know who you are," she began to read, "but thank you for singing last night. You may not have realized it, but you were singing to me. I was ready to end my life, to check out for good, but then you started to sing, 'When you walk through a storm hold your head up high and you'll never walk alone.'

You saved my life. You helped me to see myself as someone significant. I'm going to another town to follow up on a job there, and start my life again. You made it possible. I wanted you to know how important a part of my life you are. Thank you. Good-bye."

There it was, the ripple effect and how those ripples can produce rainbows, ripples which can produce rainbows in the lives of others. There was my message to suit my title. Little did this lady know the effect, the ripple effect so to speak, that her actions would have on the life of the man of whom she had been afraid. Little did she know how, through her actions, she would create a rainbow in the life of this man. Often a simple smile, a song sung from the heart, or a simple word of encouragement, a small ripple, if you will, can be the light which will create a rainbow in the life of another. The light we emit is indeed important. Listen again to our Scripture reading for today: "You are the light of the world. A city built on a hill cannot hide. No one after lighting a lamp puts it under the bushel basket, but on the lamp stand, and it gives light to all in the house. In the same way, let your light shine before others, so that they may see your good works and give glory to your Father in heaven."

Friends it is important that we make our light shine. It is important not only for our own happiness but for the happiness of others. Through our actions, we can produce ripples of hope, ripples of trust, ripples of joy, ripples of happiness. We never know how the tiniest ripple, a ripple caused by just one small step, or one small, but positive action, may spread and reverberate to the point that we create rainbows in the lives of others.

William Barclay had this to say about Matthew 5:14 where Jesus proclaimed, "You are the light of the world." This, he said, is the greatest compliment ever paid to the individual Christian to be what Jesus claimed to be in John 9:5 when he said, "While I am in the world, I am the light of the world." Jesus demanded of his followers that they should be nothing less than that; they should be like himself. Jesus set the example. Jesus died for us. It seems the least we can do is to let our light shine for the benefit of others.

There are, of course, many ways to let our light shine, many ways to turn ripples into rainbows. Jesus demonstrated how to do so. He offered sustenance to the hungry. He offered hope to the hopeless. He offered strength to the weak. He offered faith to the faithless. He made the sick well. He offered forgiveness to sinners. He offered his life that we may live.

Scott Whitacre has shared two other stories with us of people making their light shine, of turning ripples into rainbows. First, there is the story about the high school baseball game, where the pitcher struck out his best friend to win the game for his team. While his teammates ran to each other to celebrate their win, this pitcher ran immediately to his best friend, who had struck out to lose the game for his team, to hug him and console him on his loss? "It just felt like the right thing to do," the pitcher said.

Then, there is the story of two young ladies who had been friends most of their lives and who were competing for the 2000 Summer Olympic games in the sport of taek won do. They were both excellent fighters, and they both made it through the many rounds of the tryouts, never having to compete against each other, only to find that both of them made it to the final round and would compete against each other to see who would be selected to go to the Olympics. Just prior to the final round, one of the young ladies had suffered a severe leg injury in the match just prior to the final round, but she knew she had to engage in this final fight in order to have a chance to go to the Olympics. Her friend knew of this injury and could well have taken advantage of it. As they both entered the ring, the young friend who had not been hurt, as the fight was about to begin, bowed to her opponent. Everyone watching knew what this meant. She had yielded the fight to her young friend, knowing that her friend was the better fighter, and she chose not to take advantage of her injury. She stayed home and her friend went on to the Olympics. Winston Churchill said, "We make a living by what we get. We make a life by what we give."

Our gifts to others may be nothing more than a smile, an embrace, or a handwritten letter to a friend, instead of an email, letting them know what their friendship means to us, or nothing less than giving of our own riches, our own advantages, our own safety, or even our own wellbeing that others may be enriched through our contributions to them. The sharing of our own light, that ripples may turn into rainbows.

Just two or three weeks after visiting my brother, I was traveling with our son, Heath, and son-in-law, Matt, in our small boat across the Atlantic to the Bahamas. Heath snapped a picture of me as I sat relaxing in my beanbag chair in the stern of our boat. He then showed me the photo which caused me to stand in amazement to look behind me to see above the waves a beautiful rainbow. I sent the picture to our other son, Cater, who had stayed home and who knew of the title I was considering for this sermon. He immediately emailed back, "Look Dad, Ripples and Rainbows." My initial inspiration for this sermon had been reaffirmed.

I had now come full circle from my initial visit with my brother. I once again contemplated the meaning of that initial vision of the ripples in the pool and the magnificent rainbow my wife and I had seen that day.

What had all this meant to me? What would it mean to my brother? What does it mean to you? There is one thing certain, as represented by the rainbow. God has made a covenant with us that God will always be with us. Although we are not guaranteed a life free of disappointment, sorrow, or pain, we are guaranteed of God's presence and through the resurrection of Jesus Christ, hope for better days to come. And, we are assured that even the smallest ripple can produce a rainbow in the lives of others and in our own lives. Friends, remember, you are the light of the world. Always, always let your light shine. Amen.

For Those with Eyes to See
Matthew 13:1-17

Listen for God's Word

> *"'Happy are your eyes because they see.'"*
> Matthew 13:16a

Spider webs have a way of popping up seemingly out of nowhere, sometimes in places where you least expect to see them. Indeed, sometimes you don't see them at all and you walk right into them getting the sticky web on your face and hair, hoping the spider itself has not crawled somewhere onto your body.

These webs are irritating whenever they appear around your house and yard and I find the best way to get rid of them is by sweeping them away with a broom. That is exactly what I intended to do with the spider web that appeared on our back porch recently after my wife Leslie and I had been away for a few days. Until I got up close and took a good look at this particular web. I was so impressed that I was compelled to take a photograph. Have you ever seen anything in nature more perfect? Can you imagine how the tiny spider making its home in the center of this web constructed these 30 to 35 concentric circles bisected into approximately 25 equal pie shaped pieces coming together at the center of the spider's home, forming the lair in which it would trap its food? I was so impressed that I had to photograph the web and send it to many relatives and friends. I titled my photograph, "God's Handiwork." Barbara Brown Taylor, one of my friends to whom I sent the photo, dubbed it the "Sacred Web" and reminded me how God's miracles are everywhere, "for those with eyes to see."

My thanks to Barbara Brown Taylor for giving me the title to my sermon today and my thanks for the reminder of how God reveals God's self in the common places of our lives. We need only have the eyes to see.

When was the last time you came upon a spider web and thought of it as sacred? When was the last time you thought to preserve a spider web for the Godliness it represents? When was the last time your eyes were opened to the commonplace beauty of God which surrounds us every day?

I suspect you have reveled in the beauty of a sunset, a starry sky, a full moon, or a luxurious garden. But, there is so much more for us to observe if only we have the eyes to see. But, unfortunately, somehow things get in our way and either obstruct our vision or distract it to a subject less rewarding.

Just as occurred in the days of the prophet Jeremiah, where God's power as creator of all that surrounds us was not acknowledged by the people of Israel and where it was therefore written in Jeremiah chapter five, "Listen, you foolish and senseless people, who have eyes but don't see and ears but don't hear. They don't say in their hearts, Let's fear the Lord our God, who provides rain in autumn and spring and who assures us of a harvest in its season. Your wrongdoing has turned these blessings away. Your sin has robbed you of good."

The Bible is replete with such references. In Psalm chapter 115, verses 4-7, we read that the idols of the people are silver and gold, the work of human hands because they have eyes but do not see. In Ezekiel 12:2, we read "Human one, you live in a household of rebels. They have eyes to see but they don't see." In Isaiah 6:9-10 we hear the voice of the Lord exclaiming that his people keep looking but do not understand. Finally, in the New Testament in Matthew 13:15-17 it is said of the people, "You will indeed listen, but never understand, and you will indeed look, but never perceive. For this people's heart has grown dull . . . and they have shut their eyes; so that they might not look with their eyes . . . and understand with their heart."

Of course all those passages are speaking of faith or, more accurately, the lack of faith of a people whose idols are described as silver and gold, who worship the work of human hands, who do not credit God for the rain and the harvest, whose hearts have grown dull, who have shut their eyes so that they might not look with their eyes. I too speak of faith when I speak of "those with eyes to see." How can one not have faith if one's eyes are truly opened to the miracles which surround us every day? As, for example, the miracle of this spider web and the tiny spider which from its body wove this web. If we do not have the eyes to see this miracle then, I submit, as has been stated throughout the Old and New Testaments that our hearts have grown dull, that we have shut our eyes, that silver and gold and that which it can buy and that which it represents, have become a greater priority in our life. And, that although we have eyes, we do not see.

Barbara Brown Taylor, named by Time Magazine as one of the one hundred most influential people in the world and who has previously been acclaimed as one of the twelve most effective preachers in the English speaking world, who will be addressing you from this pulpit in January, has addressed this topic in her book, *An Altar in the World*, which I would commend to each of you for reading. In the book she reveals how to see the sacred in our everyday lives. One of these ways, she says, is to pay attention. The practice of paying attention, she says, takes time. "Most of us move so quickly that our surroundings become no more than the blurred scenery we fly past on our way to somewhere else," she says. "We pay attention to the speedometer, the wristwatch, the cell phone, the list of all the things we have to do. No one has time to lie on the deck watching stars, or to wonder how one's hand came to be, or to see the soul of a stranger walking by. The artist, Georgia O'Keefe, who became famous for her sensuous paintings of flowers, explained her success by saying, 'In a way, nobody sees a flower, really, it is so small, we haven't time – and to see takes time.'"

Those who have eyes to see take the time to see. That is important. In order to take time to see it is important that, from time to time, we take our eyes off those things which occupy our time which keep us from viewing those miracles which surround us every day. I am reminded of a T-shirt I saw in a store in Canada last summer, which I wish I had purchased. It said, "Let's go someplace really cool this weekend and stare at our cell phones." You laugh, but oh how true that is and how unfortunate that our vision of the world around us is blurred by such distractions. Distractions which cause us to take our eyes off the road in more ways than one.

It is my belief that if we can discipline ourselves to rid ourselves of distractions which prevent us from seeing, if we open our eyes to see the miracle of the ordinary, we will have eyes to see the extraordinary miracles that we may never have noticed before. I know there are those of you here who have seen and experienced such miracles. I know also that to see and experience those miracles, you first had to have the eyes to see, as well as the heart and the faith to believe.

Anne Lamott, in her book, *Travelling Mercies*, writes of an experience she had in her bedroom in the midst of a depressed state of mind when she was seeking more for her life than what life was offering her at the time. She wrote, "After a while as I lay there I became aware of someone with me hunkered down in the corner. After a while more, I knew beyond a doubt that it was Jesus. I felt him just sitting there on his haunches in the corner of my sleeping loft, watching me with patience and love and I squinted my eyes shut but that didn't help because that's not what I was seeing him with."

It was not with her eyes that she was seeing. It was with her heart and through her faith. Some might argue that what she saw was a figment of her imagination but, clearly, it was not to her and, as a result, what she saw changed her life.

I submit your life and mine can also be changed if we will allow ourselves the time and opportunity to see, not only with our eyes but also with our hearts.

Allow me to conclude with a personal story. It is about someone who I know very well. Indeed, it involves two people I know well. The woman was awakened one night for a reason she could not explain. She sat up in bed to look around for she felt there was something strange in the hallway outside her daughter's bedroom. She saw something in the hallway but could not make it out. Like Anne Lamott she squinted her eyes, then rubbed them, but what she saw did not go away. It just hovered outside her daughter's bedroom. She went back to sleep. When she woke up the vision she had seen outside her daughter's bedroom was gone but it did not leave her mind. She was bothered by it, so she cancelled the tennis game she had scheduled and cancelled the sitter she had arranged to stay with her daughter. Suddenly, her daughter, just three months old, became very sick. The mother immediately rushed her daughter to the hospital where, after some testing, she was diagnosed with bacterial spinal meningitis, an often-deadly disease and, more often than not, a disease which leaves its victims with permanent mental or physical disabilities. Because of the mother's quick response, her daughter's life was not only spared but she had no lasting effects from this normally devastating disease. Had the mother's eyes not been opened to what she had seen from her bed that night, she would not have stayed home and would not have been there to take care of her daughter who has grown into a beautiful young lady with a family of her own to watch over, just as her mother did her. And, as does her mother, she too has eyes to see.

It was not with her eyes that she was seeing. It was with her heart and through her faith. Some might argue that what she saw was a figment of her imagination but, clearly, it was not to her and, as a result, what she saw changed her life.

I submit your life and mine can also be changed if we will allow ourselves the time and opportunity to see, not only with our eyes but also with our hearts.

I shall be forever grateful to my wife who had the eyes to see the angel that appeared that night outside our daughter's bedroom and to God for having saved the life of our daughter those many years ago.

My spider web is gone now. I had intended to save my little miracle for as long as I could, to share it with others and to observe the activities of the spider in its web. But, the next day it was gone, swept away by the yardmen who were doing what they do best, keeping my yard clean and neat.

There would be more such miracles, I thought. If only I pay attention, if only I use my heart and my faith, as well as my eyes. If only I have eyes to see. Amen.

The Day Christ Came to Town
Matthew 6:5-8

Listen for God's Word

"But when you pray, go to your room, shut the door,
and pray to your Father who is present in that secret place."
Matthew 6:6

The news spread slowly at first. It began as an obscure news item, a short paragraph found buried on Page 23C of the local newspaper. It was something like those articles we frequently read where some group or individual predicts the end of the world on a certain date. In fact, at first the reaction to this news was quite the same as it usually is to those "world comes to end" stories. No one really believed it, although it did arouse the curiosity and amusement of many people.

The strange thing about this news article though, was that no one knew where the news originated. It wasn't even quoted from one of those reliable sources with which we are all so familiar in political circles. It was a simple statement and it appeared strangely with no one from the newspaper claiming knowledge of its source. It said simply, *"The Lord Jesus Christ Shall Walk Among You."*

Slowly the story started to be expounded upon. The amusement and curiosity became less prevalent and there was something of an air of cautious belief. Cautious, at least at first, in that those who began to believe something was going to happen would not admit it outwardly. Things changed quickly, however. Maybe it was because they wanted to believe that this story began taking hold at an ever-quickening pace. Soon people became outwardly excited, more and more admitting they believed the story, and that it was going to happen. Somehow, a date was established, a particular day was chosen as the day Christ would come to town. These are the stories of the lives and events of certain people on that day.

Bill and Penny Loudon were somewhat preoccupied that day. They were honeymooning in Delray Beach. It was the first trip to the area for both of them, their home being in the Midwestern United States. Neither had ventured far from home prior to this occasion. Their minds were not on the newspaper this day but they couldn't help become aware, because of the wide publicity it had received, of the news that Jesus Christ was coming. The Loudons fell somewhere in between being casually interested and not caring about this news. At any rate, they weren't about to sit around and wait for the event and they didn't care to go to any of the parades or rallies which were scheduled in celebration of the coming of Christ. Heading for the beach was all they had in mind that morning. Neither had ever seen the ocean before. As others awaited the arrival of Christ, these two frolicked on the white beach sand, interested only in the laughter and love they shared together, admiring on occasion the rush of the waves, the sounds of the seagulls and the staccato walk of the sandpipers foraging for their food. They delighted at the dolphin playing a few yards beyond the breaking surf, and they felt aglow themselves in the radiance of the purple sky at sunset. As their day ended, full as it was, neither had given any thought about Christ and whether he had come that day.

While others prepared excitedly for the arrival of Christ, Tom Marston prepared for another arrival, that of his first child. He too had heard of the impending visit of Christ, and although he was interested, he hardly had time to make any special arrangements. His day started early at 2 a.m. when his wife Gloria complained of her first signs of labor. The pains were infrequent at first and irregular. Tom, having taken a course in childbirth with his wife, remained calm, knowing there was still some time before he had to rush off to the hospital. During that time, while he helped Gloria get her things together, he did some reflecting. He reflected on the time he first learned that Gloria was pregnant and how that news had brought the two of them closer together. He reflected on the change of their activities, how they now did more together, the childbirth course, the shopping for items for the baby, and generally more family related activities. He reflected on the time Gloria placed his hand on her stomach and how he felt for the first time the kick of life from inside her womb, and how they thrilled at that occasion. Tom was suddenly awakened from his reflective mood by Gloria who was now experiencing more frequent pain and was ready for the trip to the hospital. Tom was allowed into the delivery room to observe and assist in the delivery of his own child, an experience he would never forget. This was one time that the realization was much greater than the anticipation which preceded the event. He held Gloria's hand tightly as the baby was delivered. Tears welled in his eyes as he first observed their newborn child and he delighted at the shriek of happiness from his wife when they learned it was a girl. He stared as though hypnotized at that little creature as she breathed her first breath and cried her first cry.

It had been an overwhelming experience for Tom that day, a full and busy day which began early and ended late because of the excitement which followed the birth. As Tom finally paused at day's end, he wondered for a moment if Christ had come to town that day.

Still others waited for the visitation of Christ. Paul and Harriett Lambert were good Christians. They had been all their lives, sixty-five years of those lives having been spent together as husband and wife. They were quite excited about the prospect of seeing Jesus Christ this day. They were a little too old and a little too tired to attempt to participate in any of the affairs scheduled in anticipation of this event, and they were a little disappointed they couldn't get out, thinking they might miss the chance to see Jesus Christ. Who was to say that Christ would not come to see them, to pay a special visit? After all, they had attended church faithfully for these past sixty-five years. Harriett tidied up the house in anticipation of the possible visit. She and Paul sat together hand in hand that day, becoming more fully convinced as each hour passed that Christ would pay them a visit. As they sat, they occupied their time looking at their family photo album. There was their son Bob's baby pictures, Bob now grown and with a family of his own, living in California. Sally, their daughter, had surprised them all and had gone to medical school and had become a successful practitioner. Oh, how happy they were for their successes. Their reflections of years gone by provided them a feeling of warmth and accomplishment that they had not felt in a long time. As they waited together, they reminisced and they did not feel sad but felt instead a deep sense of fulfillment. The day wore on and it grew late so Paul and Harriett Lambert decided to turn in. They were disappointed that they had not seen Christ that day. But, the day had not been a total loss, for on that day, more than on any day before, they felt a complete sense of satisfaction and fulfillment with their lives.

The day was drawing to a close now. There were no reports of anyone having seen Jesus Christ. The last of the cleaning crews retired for the day, having cleaned up from the various parades and celebrations held for the coming of the Savior. But, he failed to show, they said. The newspapers went to press that night with this headline: *"Christ Fails to Appear."*

That night, shortly before midnight, Willy Reynolds was getting ready to retire on his favorite park bench. Willy had not heard that Christ was supposed to have come to town that day. He did not often see the newspapers unless he salvaged one from someone's trash bin located in the various alleys throughout the downtown area. His eyes were bleary and bloodshot from too much drink again that day. It hadn't always been like that. No one really knew the full story behind Willy. Suffice it to say he had suffered, so greatly in fact that he had been driven from the pinnacles of financial and social success to the pits of despair, and each day now was drowned in drink and memories of happy days gone by. As was his custom, before going to sleep, Willy knelt in front of his park bench and prayed this simple prayer: "Thank you Lord Jesus for being with me through yet another day."

As Willy rose from his knees beside the park bench, he was startled as he saw a strange, dark figure standing before him. The stranger put his hand on Willy's shoulder and Willy stood speechless as the figure began to speak.

"Willy, I can always count on you. You have surely suffered, in a greater degree than most of my Father's children. But, each day you are aware of my presence and each day you give thanks for those blessings that have been bestowed upon you. How happy I would be if there were more like you. I have had a busy day, Willy. I spent the day with a young couple, just married, and blessed with a fresh love for each other. I shared with them today some of the magnificence of our Father's world. I showed them the majesty of the sea, the beauty of God's creatures, the brilliance of a sunset, the joy of laughter, the warmth of being together in union under God.

It made me happy to be with them this day. But, I am saddened, Willy. Because with all that, they were not aware of my presence and not one thought was given to our Father in heaven in thanks for that day.

"I also spent the day with a new young father. That is always one of my most satisfying experiences, through our Father in heaven, breathing the breath of life into another child of God, creating a new life. Of all the miracles, Willy, that is surely one of the greatest.

"It is almost beyond imagination. Think about it for a moment. From the love of two people, another life is formed and it lives and breathes and has its being.

"I spent the entire day with that young man. I shared with him the joy of life, from the conception to the birth itself which he observed. And you know, Willy, after the day was over, that young man wondered where I was. I am saddened by this.

"My day was also spent with an elderly couple who sat prepared for my coming. I made them aware of their lives' fulfillment, of all they had accomplished by God's grace, and still they waited and they went to sleep wondering why I had not come.

"I am saddened by all of this, Willy. Even though people were prepared for my coming on this day, they did not recognize my presence. Though I shared with them today the blessings of our Father's Kingdom, at day's end they still stood in wait for me and wondered why I had not come. They went to bed saying I had not appeared.

"Why are people not aware of my continued presence? Why are they not prepared each day for my coming? Why should it be that elaborate preparations are made on one particular day with the thought in mind that I may come to walk among you? Attitudes and behaviors should not be adjusted to prepare for that day because each person should be prepared each day for my coming, for I am with you each day. You have delighted me, Willy. Here you are, amidst your plight and suffering, aware of my daily presence, and thankful for it. Because of your love for me, I have disclosed myself to you.

"It is because of the lack of that love and faith, even though my presence is abiding always, that it is not disclosed to others. Although I was present today in the lives of these other people, my presence was not manifested in them. It was not disclosed to them because their love and faith has not reached the degree necessary for them to know of my presence.

"The Scriptures read: 'I will not leave you bereft. I am coming back to you. Because I live, you too will live; then you will know that I am in my Father, and you in me and I in you. He who loves me will be loved by my Father; and I will love him and disclose myself to him.'

Not until love prevails in my Father's Kingdom will my presence be disclosed."

As swiftly as he had appeared, the dark figure was gone. Willy was asleep by now, his rumpled coat serving as a pillow for his head on the hard bench. When he awoke the next morning, Willy wiped the sleep from his eyes and reflected momentarily on what had seemed to be a dream. As he looked around, he saw beside him a newspaper. It was the morning newspaper, the same one that had gone to press the night before with the headline *"Christ Fails to Appear."*

Something strange had happened to that newspaper, something no one could explain. Willy picked it up, slowly unfolded it and read this headline out loud: *"Lo, I Am With You Always, Even Unto The End Of The Age."* Amen.

Afterword
Reading Sermons Devotionally

"Every Scripture is inspired by God and is useful for teaching, for showing mistakes, for correcting, and for training character, so that the person who belongs to God can be equipped to do everything that is good."
2 Timothy 3:16, 17

I ordered a cookbook once. I was eighteen years old and entering my freshman year of college, where I would cook for myself and do my own laundry for the first time. I knew only how to prepare frozen pizza, simple salads, and cereal. I had no culinary skills. I researched online a few cookbooks for beginners, and I found the perfect book for me. The moment the book arrived in the mail, I cracked open the cover, peeled through its pages, and excitedly looked at all the dishes I'd soon be able to create.

We packed all my belongings into the back of my mom's SUV and drove to my dorm room two hours north of home. I packed my TV, the PlayStation, a chest full of clothes, some odds and ends, and a box of books. After my parents left, I carefully arranged all my books along the bookcase provided by the school, and I gave the new cookbook a prominent place on the shelf. I thought it made me look sophisticated. That first night, I was too tired to cook, so I purchased a sandwich from a local shop up the street. The school hosted the freshmen for an orientation dinner my second night on campus. By my third night, classes were already in session, and I had a mountain of reading before me.

I never did use that cookbook. I prepared plenty of frozen pizza, simple salads, and cereal though. I think I still have the cookbook, somewhere. It's unused. I've purchased other cookbooks since, and I've used about half of them, maybe. This is what I've learned from my experience with cookbooks: no matter how appetizing the dishes look or how simple the recipes appear, a cookbook is of no use if you do not use it to cook!

What you are holding is a cookbook. Each sermon you just read was designed to teach you about God and equip you with the tools needed to nurture and sustain a life of faith. You have a choice to make. You can read these sermons in a way that keeps God at a distance: you can read the recipes, look at the pictures, then set the book aside and move on with your life. Or, you can bring each sermon to bear upon the kitchen of your heart. You can chew on every word, digest these sermons, and feed your soul.

I suggest you do the latter. This begins by treating each sermon like a conversation with God. In his book *Life with God*, Richard Foster suggests when we approach God, we "bring our whole selves, expectantly, attentively, and humbly." When you approach God expectantly, you open yourself to change. You expect to be changed, because you know who God is, and you know God is in the business of changing people. Foster also suggests we approach God attentively. So often when we pray, all we do is speak, but approaching God attentively means we must listen as well. If I were inattentive to my spouse, our relationship would naturally deteriorate. The same is true of our relationships with God. There is no substitute for time spent together. Finally, each conversation with God requires a degree of humility. In Isaiah 55, God reminds us that God's ways are not our ways, nor do God's plans always mirror our own. Sometimes we hear very clearly what God wants of us, but unless we are willing to submit to God, we will not change. When we approach God with expectancy, attention, and humility, we allow God's word to transform us from the inside out.

You can begin your conversations with God by asking a few basic questions. These questions do not belong to me; I first heard them from Doug Hood. The first question is, *What, O God, would you have me hear?* The second, *What, O God, would you have me do?* I encourage you to ask these questions of each of the sermons you just read and also of future sermons you may hear.

You likely are familiar with the saying *you are what you eat*. The same is true with faith. By asking these two questions and by spending time with God, you will sustain a healthy spiritual diet. You will experience changes in your body as you slowly begin to transform into the person God made you to be. Your heart will soften. You'll smile more. God will be more alive for you than ever before. You will start to notice God in the most surprising places. And, everywhere you go, life will taste a little bit richer, and a little bit sweeter. Bon Appétit.

Greg Rapier